COWBOYS, KIDS, & CRITTERS

BY JEANETTE BARTHLE

WITH ILLUSTRATIONS BY JERRY PALEN

Parts of this book were previously published in a condensed version in *The Independent Farmer and Rancher/The Record*, Gainesville, Florida.

ISBN 1-879894-04-1 paperback

For more copies of this book or more information please write to: Jeanette Barthle, 26500 Bayhead Road, Dade City, Florida 33525

DEDICATION

For my cowboy—Joe.

TABLE OF CONTENTS

The First Cowboy

Never, even in my most vivid flights of fancy, had I imagined that I would marry a cattle rancher, have seven children, and, literally, live in the middle of nowhere!

Back in the seventh grade my English teacher, Mrs. Trotman, noted on one of my essays, "You should consider a career in writing."

Of such trivial things, dreams are born.

After that I had a latent desire to become a journalist, more specifically a newspaper reporter who would have an exciting career dashing all over the city, state, nation and, yes, even the world, writing about great events: life, death, crimes, and politics.

But reality set in. Since college seemed a financial impossibility, I prepared for an office job by taking all the secretarial courses offered at our high school. Shorthand, typing, bookkeeping and office management were fun, and easy enough for me to enjoy, while doing quite well in the subjects.

For a while I considered the possibility of becoming an airline stewardess; as flight attendants were being called at that time. But my five feet, one and a half inches didn't meet the necessary height requirements. I had to forego what I envisioned to be a glamorous and exciting career, letting me travel to interesting and exotic places.

Then a small, unexpected inheritance from an aunt made it possible for me to attend college. I applied and was accepted at Florida State University in Tallahassee.

At FSU in 1947 we were permitted to enroll in our major during the Freshman year. I quite naturally chose Journalism. Part of our out-of-class assignment was to work as a reporter for the school newspaper.

At that point all I had learned about writing a news story was to make sure that the first or "lead" paragraph contained *who, what, when, where* and *why*.

Needless to say, I was filled with both excitement and

with apprehension when I received my first assignment to write a story about a new faculty member. I wasn't too sure about the proper procedure but I did know one thing, I had to make an appointment with him. That was my first step.

Prior to World War II, FSU had been Florida State College for Women and had an all-female enrollment, while its sister institution, the University of Florida, was all-male. By 1947 both institutions had turned coed and FSU had a sprinkling of male students.

FSU had been enlarged and divided into two campuses to accommodate the increased enrollment, many of whom were veterans. East Campus, the original one, had lovely old brick dormitories, buildings covered with ivy, and streets that were lined with large trees draped with long gray strands of Spanish moss. West Campus, located miles away at a former Army camp, was typical of a military base, stark and unadorned. The original army Quonset huts and army barracks were covered in a drab gray coat of paint. Some classes were held in these buildngs, but they were used mostly as housing for married veterans.

With boys enrolled, FSU fielded its first football team that Fall of 1947. What the Seminoles lacked in experience and winning ability was more than compensated for by the exuberance and school spirit of the students, alumni and fans.

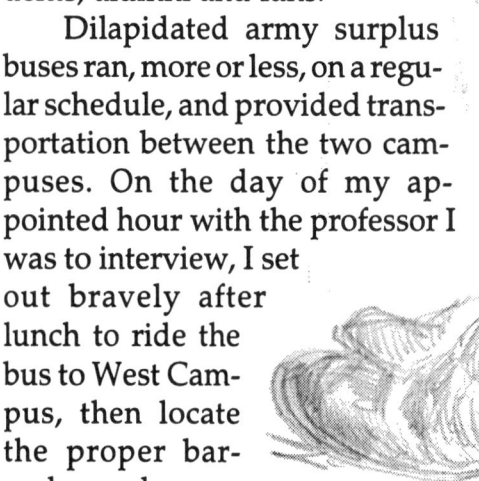

Dilapidated army surplus buses ran, more or less, on a regular schedule, and provided transportation between the two campuses. On the day of my appointed hour with the professor I was to interview, I set out bravely after lunch to ride the bus to West Campus, then locate the proper barracks and room where my subject was, I hoped, awaiting my arrival. He was indeed there, and after completing the interview I returned to the dorm to write my story.

I don't recall with any great clarity how long that story was nor what it said, but I do vividly remember my feelings as I searched for and finally found it in the paper. At that moment I had my first ego-deflating experience. There was my work, cut to one paragraph! It very concisely stated who had done what, when and where he had done it, and why he had done it.

Humbling as the experience was, it was a thrill to see in print what was supposed to be my work and it encouraged me to continue to prepare for bigger and better writing opportunities. I was sure that I was finally on the way to a successful career as a journalist!

Then I met Joe Barthle - my first cowboy!

When I met him, it never crossed my mind that this young cowboy would alter the course of my life and change my plans for the future so completely.

Dade City, where I grew up with my widowed mother and older sister, Ruby, is a small town in West Central Florida. Joe was raised in the even smaller town of San Antonio, six miles to the west. He lived in what was really just a village with his parents, his younger brother Albert and three older sisters: Mary, Margaret, and Ruth.

San Antonio was, and still is, a predominantly Catholic community. In the 1940's Protestants and Catholics still tended to mingle in their social activities with people of their own faith. That, and the fact that Joe is almost five years my senior, had made it unlikely that we would meet socially while I was still in high school.

So, despite the fact that we had been born and raised within six miles of each other, our paths had never happened to cross. It took my college roommate to bring us together.

After graduation from high school a group of girls, accompanied by chaperones, traveled to Amherst, Massachusetts, to live on campus and work as imported labor on the tobacco farms. One member of the group, Anne Scudder, was from San Antonio. We got to know each other that summer and arranged to room together at FSU.

Between classes, football games, and other assorted activities of college life, the first semester passed by quickly and pleasantly. Then during Christmas vacation I spent a weekend with Anne in San Antonio.

On Sunday morning we joined the young people of St. Anthony parish for a Sodality breakfast. The girls served the meal to the boys and as I helped them one of the young men caught my eye. As girls will, I flirted with him a little and must have gotten his attention because he returned the teasing and left a tip for me. A penny!

I've always maintained that he got a good bargain for his money. Others have suggested that the result he got from that penny either soured him forever on tipping or he considered it the best investment he ever made. Joe has never committed himself either way.

Later that morning, after we had returned to her home, Anne, who was dating Albert, said to me, "I'm going to try to arrange a double date with Joe for you."

"Okay," I replied. "It's all right with me."

I wasn't too surprised when a few minutes later the doorbell rang and there stood this lean, lanky cowboy, with a grin on his face, asking me for a date. That cowboy has never needed anyone to play John Alden for him!

Our first date was a double date with Anne and Albert. We drove forty miles to have dinner at the Columbia Restaurant, a beautiful, elegant historical landmark in Ybor City, the Latin section of Tampa. As I suspect Joe intended me to be, I was duly impressed.

Our second date came a few days later when we went to a rodeo on New Year's Eve. Joe was entered in the calf roping and steer wrestling, known in the vocabulary of rodeo people as "bulldogging" or just "dogging."

He was "up" in the dogging at that performance and wanted to show off for his new girlfriend by making a good throw and winning the "go-round." What he didn't realize was that I was watching my first rodeo and wouldn't know good from bad!

When his turn came Joe and his hazer carefully positioned themselves on their horses in the boxes on either side of the chute where the steer waited to be turned out. At a nod from Joe the gate snapped open and the steer came out running.

The two cowboys got out of the chutes just right. They rode up well, one on either side of the steer, and the hazer kept him running in a straight line while Joe positioned himself for his jump.

Leaning over from his saddle, Joe made a good jump, grabbed the steer by the horns, and dug the heels of his boots into the ground as he threw his weight back to stop the steer and throw him onto his side with all four legs straight out.

Everything was done perfectly, by the book, in record time. Only one thing went wrong: the steer had gotten his legs square under him and he wouldn't fall!

That steer dragged that cowboy all over the arena before Joe was finally able to bring him to a halt and make the throw in forty-three seconds—too long a time! He was embarrassed but I thought that he had "done good."

A few months later when I went to another rodeo with him Joe was again up in the dogging. That time things went better for him. He got his steer down in just over five seconds and won!

The Christmas holidays were soon over. Anne and I returned to FSU, a good five-hour trip by bus.

Joe and I corresponded but didn't see each other again until summer vacation. During the summer our friendship grew. Then our romance blossomed. By the time I returned to Tallahassee the next Fall, we were unofficially engaged!

FROM THE BEGINNING

Acquiring land and starting a ranch operation was much easier and much less expensive in the 1930's when the Barthle Ranch was formed. It wasn't necessary to contend with the permits, rules and regulations, environmentalists, animal rightists, and so on that we're faced with today.

Joseph Albert Barthle (also known as Joe) was born in North Dakota. His family moved to Florida in 1897 when he was 12 years old. They settled in San Antonio where they owned and operated the St. Charles Hotel for many years.

San Antonio was, and still is, a small village near the even smaller community of St. Joseph to which many other Barthles had already, or would later, emigrate.

The history of the Barthle clan in the area is somewhat curious and dates back to my husband's great-grandfather's three marriages. He had a son by each of his three wives. From those three half-brothers the present Barthle families are descended, "filling the woods," so to speak, with Barthles.

Trying to untangle the relationships between all of the families can be a frustrating procedure, especially to a newcomer such as I was when I married into the third generation of this clan. One has to take into account all of the grandparents, aunts, uncles, nieces, nephews, and cousins that are once, twice, or three-times removed, keeping in mind that many are "half-cousins."

The fact that there were several other large families in the area and that they all intermarried really adds to the complications of determining whose relations are whose!

Joe Barthle, Sr. was an astute business man. At one time or another, he had business interests which included a sawmill, grocery store, and, in the 1920's, a road construction company.

The sophisticated road-building equipment used now wasn't, of course, invented then; all his equipment was powered by mules. Many roads were graded and built up, but not paved. Although road construction was a money-making business, Joe Barthle went out of the business overnight.

He and his crew had just completed a road in Georgia and he was scheduled to turn it over to the state the next day. Mother Nature stepped in with a torrential rain storm and the road was washed out while still under his contract. Repairing the road wiped out his resources, so he turned to another endeavor. . .Cattle.

In the 1930's Florida still had open cattle range. Cattle moved where and when they wished to graze, but the herds stayed within a fairly well-defined area bounded by privately fenced areas and cattle guards to keep them out of the cities and towns.

Even so, raising cattle entailed a lot of horseback riding, especially to inspect the herds regularly for screw worms. If an animal was found to be infected, it was roped and doctored on the spot.

During the Fall of the year the herds were rounded up, trailed for six or seven miles, and penned. They were then marked, branded, and neutered and the steers and old cows were separated to be marketed.

Once the "Fence Law" was enacted in the late 1930's cattle had to be fenced in to keep them off the roads, the railroad tracks, and other people's property. It was at that time that Joe Barthle began to acquire rangeland of his own on which to pasture his cattle.

"Turpentining" was big business in the area. Turpentine and rosin companies bought up large tracts of land with heavy stands of long needle pine trees. Crews then went through the woods making a large V-shaped slash on the trunk of each pine tree, sometimes one on each side if the tree was very large, to bleed the tree of pine sap or rosin. Below the slash. they fastened a tin cup. The pine sap, or rosin, would drip out of the slash and into the cup. The crews periodically collected the sap and removed a new strip of bark from which more sap could seep.

Once the turpentine company completed the collection process, they usually sold the tract of land. The Barthles took advantage of this turnover.

My Joe always enjoys telling how his father, Joe Barthle

Sr., acquired one 7500 acre tract of land. As his lawyer, George Dayton, who accompanied Mr. Barthle that day, related it to Joe many years later, the story went like this:

Mr. Barthle had an agreement with the turpentine company to purchase the 7500 acres. He and George made the long drive to Jacksonville to meet with the directors of the company and close the deal. As the meeting proceeded, one wise old director stated, "I think we should have the timber on the land cruised [have the timber value estimated] before we sell it."

Mr. Barthle was a man of few words. He stood up and calmly told the directors, "Gentlemen. I came up here to close this deal today. If you want to do it, fine. If you don't, good day."

As he started to leave the other directors hastened to assure him, "Oh, no, Mr. Barthle. Wait. We *want* to close this deal today."

They proceeded with the closing of the deal. For the sum of $12,000, he had 7500 acres to add to the ranch he was putting together.

George always paused and laughed heartily before he delivered the punch line. "What the directors didn't know was that your Daddy had a tentative contract in his pocket to sell the timber on the land for enough money to pay for it!"

Bit by bit he acquired additional parcels of land to make up the 18,000 acres that formed the J.A. Barthle and Sons Ranch: a wilderness of raw pasture, cypress ponds, oak scrubs, palmettos, cabbage palms, ponds, and lakes. This was a land abounding with wildlife, rattlesnakes, and birds of many kinds, and its lakes and ponds were teeming with fish and water-fowl.

A LONG RIDE

My first visit to the "Barthle U Ranch - JA. Barthle and Sons" occurred after dark. It was my first meeting with Joe's parents and I was anticipating it with pleasure. The little bit of nagging apprehension I felt turned out to be unnecessary because they greeted me very warmly and made me feel more than welcome.

As Joe drove me from Dade City and the road unfurled before us in the moonlight, I was able to catch glimpses of the dark shapes of cattle in the fenced pastures as the fence posts flashed by in regular rhythm on either side of the road.

Though the ranch was only fifteen miles from town, the trip that first time seemed endless. The trek began on seven miles of a very narrow paved road, what we call a "hard" road. That part wasn't too bad, but from there the road regressed to a scarified section, a hard road that had been chopped up, probably because it had become filled with too many pot holes to be repaired. The last four miles or so was on a graded dirt road that was relatively smooth, at least compared to the spine-jarring scarified section.

The ranch, located right in the middle of nothing but trees and pastures, lies fifteen miles from Dade City, thirteen from San Antonio, and ten from Brooksville. Since the area does not have an official name—even yet—Joe and Albert and their friends had taken to calling it "Possum Trot Valley," probably because possums made up such a large part of the population there.

Some years later, when our oldest son was about twelve, he erected a sign by the side of the road proclaiming, "Possum Trot Valley, Population 23". He must have added in the dogs and cats to arrive at that figure because there certainly weren't that many people living here even then.

At the time of my first visit, it was a sparsely populated area. The households within a five mile radius could just about have been counted on both hands.

The day after I arrived, as ranchers so often do, Joe and his brother Albert combined work with pleasure, and we had a pleasant ride through the pastures, while searching for cases of screwworms to be doctored. That day I had my first lesson in horseback riding on a horse named Topper. He was a gentle bay gelding who was not too tall and well-mannered enough to give me not a bit of trouble that day.

One of the few things that never changed as long as I rode with Joe was that I was always mounted on a gentle horse who behaved well. I was always grateful for that because I never did become a first-class rider, nor have I ever been completely at ease on horseback.

But I was pleased to receive one compliment on my horsemanship that first day.

"A lot of people who are riding for the first time hold a rein in each hand instead of holding both of them in one hand and keeping the other hand on the saddle horn," Joe commented to me. "Where did you learn how to do it right?"

Not wishing to appear any more unknowledgeable about the big animals than was necessary, I only laughed and didn't admit that I had watched him and copied the way he held his reins. Besides that, being new at the sport and afraid that I might fall off, I wanted something to hold onto and the saddlehorn was all that was available!

Topper and I got along just fine. Later I learned that he had a favorite trick of lying down whenever he had to wade through water. He also took a perverse pleasure in turning in circles while a rider was attempting to mount. He especially liked to try that trick with Albert who was, of course, an excellent and experienced rider. For some reason he almost always stood fairly still for me. Maybe he sensed my uneasiness and was trying to be kind. I only learned later that a horse will try to take advantage of an inexperienced and nervous rider.

At that moment in the history of cattle ranching in Florida, screwworms were prevalent and one of the biggest problems ranchers faced. The flies would lay their eggs in open wounds on the animals. After the screwworms, or maggots, hatched they would quite literally eat the flesh in and around the wound. If left untreated the animal would lose weight, become ill, and eventually die.

The worms then metamorphosed into flies and the cycle was repeated. Eventually the Florida Department of Agriculture, urged on by the Florida Cattlemen's Association, eradicated the screwworm by the simple, but costly, expedient of turning loose hordes of sterile flies which, when they mated, could produce no off-spring. After a few years, the screwworm scourge died out.

While they were prevalent, though, ranchers spent many long hours on horseback, riding in the woods and pastures to find and doctor infected animals. That was that we were doing on the day I was initiated into the joys of horseback riding.

That first ride lasted for four or five hours. We rode over a large section of the ranch, scouring the oak scrubs, cypress ponds, and palmetto patches for animals who needed treatment. Long before the ride was over, my knees and other parts of my anatomy were screaming in protest.

Shifting silently in the saddle, I tried to ease the pressure on my backside without being too noticeable about it. Alternately, I would ease my feet from the stirrups and allow my legs to hang loose for a while to help the ache in my knees.

Since I wanted to make a good impression on this cowboy, I tried to keep smiling, with no complaints or whining. Inwardly my mind kept demanding, "Isn't this ride ever going to end? Aren't we ever going back? How much longer can this torture last?"

Possum trot Valley
Population 23.

Eventually the long ride was finished and we arrived back at the barn. Topper was glad to get home too, and demonstrated it by quickening his pace to a trot as we neared the barn where he knew his evening feed was waiting.

When I slid from the saddle to the ground, my legs buckled in protest and for a while I found it a little uncomfortable to stand or walk. That wasn't too bad and didn't last very long but the next day I was stiff and sore and found it a little more than difficult to sit!

Somewhere in our memorabilia there is a photo that someone took that day of me kneeling in front of Joe. Joe claims that I was proposing, but I insist that I was only pleading, "Please don't put me back on that horse!"

A NEW LIFE TOGETHER

Instead of returning to school after that Christmas vacation, I found a job as secretary and spent the next six months working while we prepared for our wedding.

It was important to me that Joe and I be members of the same church and raise our family together in that religion. One of the first things I did was to pay a visit on Father John Schmidt, O. S. B. who had baptized Joe.

Father John, then in his eighties, instructed me in the Catholic faith and baptized me. On Easter Sunday, I received my first Holy Communion from him. Fourteen months later, he baptized our first child.

Like many girls, I had cherished dreams of being a June bride. I just barely made it. On June 30, 1949, Father John officiated at our wedding in St. Rita Church in Dade City.

It was a small traditional wedding, and then we left on a honeymoon that lasted a month during which we drove 8000 miles.

Since Joe was rodeoing some on weekends, he wanted to see The Calgary Stampede in Canada. On the way we did a lot of sightseeing, including Pike's Peak, the Grand Canyon, and Yellowstone National Park.

Leaving Canada we crossed the upper United States and visited Niagara Falls, one of *my* dreams for an ideal honeymoon. It was the trip of a lifetime and it had to last us almost that long because it was twenty-five years and seven kids later before we finally were able to take another trip alone!

As we began a new life together we jokingly declared that we wanted a large family: twelve children. Nobody believed us, so we added that, in all seriousness, we would like to have six, with no preference on our part as to how many should be boys or girls.

In the early 1950's, friends, family, and acquaintances tended to count on their fingers when newlyweds showed some evidence of beginning their family "too soon" after the nuptial vows had been exchanged.

Our first little cowboy, Randy, was born eleven months—minus three days—after our wedding. Even though he waited nine days after his due date to make his appearance, the time elapsed since we said "I do" was one finger more than two hands, almost a two finger margin!

It was three years before a little cowgirl, Jan, joined her brother, followed by Steve and Kathy at two year intervals. We already had a growing crew.

Until then we had more or less planned our family and had decided that maybe four kids would be enough after all. But we had bragged and nature saw to it that we lived up to it. Thirteen months later Larry made his unscheduled debut.

Technically that gave us five children in eight years but, in actuality the last four had arrived in five years. I definitely considered that we had done our fair share to populate Mother Earth and I was ready to call it quits!

But when Mark was born four years later, followed by Beth in another four years, when Randy was almost sixteen, we were happy to have more babies in the house and they brought a great deal of happiness, not only to Joe and me, but to all of the family. Jan and Kathy especially liked having their own real live dolls!

We enjoyed raising our children, and they were our first priority. With a sixteen-year age span between Randy and Beth, we were involved in activities at all age levels—at the same time.

There were times when I wouldn't have been surprised to pass myself coming or going. I hauled kids to baseball, football, track, and basketball practice and events. There were 4-H and FFA meetings, piano and dance class and recitals, cheerleading practice, altar boy activities, swimming, roller-skating, birthday parties, picnics, campouts, and a great deal of visiting back and forth with friends.

All of the kids attended St. Anthony School throughout the eighth grade and had to be delivered and picked up each day. Another run was necessary to pick up a kindergartner at noon. Some days I made as many as four or five trips to town.

I frequently ran errands while they were occupied with their various activities, but there are just so many errands you can run! To avoid another trip to town I spent many hours sitting in the car or watching the little kids play in a park while we waited for the older ones.

I was the official chauffeur, but Joe helped when his work load allowed. We tried to arrange it so that we could both attend the kid's special activities, but sometimes that wasn't possible and we had to go in two different directions. However, at least one of us was almost always there for them.

Kids make a lot of noise. If we had lived in town the noise emanating from our house could easily have been heard for an entire city block. . . at least. With seven kids and their friends there were almost always several radios, TVs, stereos, and probably a child's record player in operation mostly, but not always, in different rooms.

Piano and guitar practice added to the din. The washer and drier, which always seemed to be in operation, and the assorted kitchen appliances necessary for feeding eleven people also contributed their share to the decibel level.

All of that doesn't even take into account the laughter and arguments, always at high volume, of children at play nor the sound of Mama yelling at them, sometimes in exasperation, sometimes just in an effort to get their attention.

In addition to Joe and me and the seven kids, our family was extended to include Grandpa (Joe's daddy) and Grandma (my mother). Each grandparent required his or her own room so, like Topsy, our house "just grew" until it became a rambling, added-on-to, thirteen-room home.

With all of those people to cook, launder, clean, and care for, the years flew by until suddenly the grandparents had passed away and all of the children were married and raising their own families.

Randy and his "Georgia Peach" Patty, were the first to be

married. Beth, who was only six, made a really sweet little flower girl. We never got past the stage of having children in the family. Because Beth was only ten when the first grandchild, Clint, arrived. Brant and Sarabeth followed and completed Randy and Patty's family.

Jan met Ed Dillard, an Alabaman, while they were both students at Auburn University. After they were married he became by extension, a Florida Cracker, too. Their little "War Eagles" are Nick, Brian, and Lauren.

Kathy married a South Florida rancher and they have a boy and a girl, Matt and Cassie.

Steve and Becky, a transplanted Arizonian, were the next to wed, followed shortly by Larry and Lynn, a native Floridian from Gainesville. Steve and Becky gave us Amanda and Joe and Larry and Lynn produced Ben, Chris and Kayla.

Mark and Tammy, a local girl, were the last to tie the knot and have three girls; Molly, Megan, and Beth.

With members of the family having attended the University of Florida, Florida State University, and Auburn University, all arch enemies on the football field, things get pretty heated up at times with snide remarks against one school or the other.

It seemed that for a while babies were constantly popping out everywhere. The oldest, Clint, was only sixteen when the sixteenth, Beth, was born. At one point in time there were ten grandchildren aged eight and under. We had wanted grandchildren, and we got them in bunches!

Joe is affectionately called "Papa Joe" by all of them but they have assorted names for me. I answer to Grammele, Gramma, Meemaw, Mimi, or whatever. So it was confusing sometimes when I signed cards to remember who called me what. I solved that problem by signing all of them "Meemaw."

As the household population decreased we began to remodel, removing some bedroom walls to make more spacious living and family rooms. We need them when the whole family congregates for holidays and the monthly birthday celebrations we have for those whose special day is in that month.

December is the only month that we don't have a birthday and Papa Joe has sole claim on November so far. Since his special day is November 26th, it usually gets combined with Thanksgiving. Sometimes he gets candles on a pie instead of a cake—which he likes better anyway!

Joe and I kinda rattle around in the empty house now and we've discussed moving into a smaller one. Somehow, though, we're not quite ready to move out and abandon all of the family memories, both good and bad, that are brought to mind by such inconsequential things as thumb tack holes in the mantle where stockings used to hang and marks on the wall where we used to measure growth.

The two spare bedrooms are still called, respectively, Uncle Mark's or Aunt Beth's room, even by the grandchildren, because Mark and Beth were the last two to use them as their own.

An Open and Shut Case

Hanging on our wall is a *COWPOKE* cartoon plaque by Ace Reid. The toe ends of a scruffy pair of cowboy boots are sticking up from a rounded grave by the side of a closed ranch gate. The epitaph on the tombstone reads, "Here lies a man that didn't close this gate."

One grizzled cowpoke is telling another, admiringly, "Gosh, the boss shore has a sense of humor."

Humorous though it is, the cartoon illustrates one of a ranch's most serious, unwritten laws: always shut it if you found it closed, or leave it open if that's the way it was when you got there.

This law doesn't apply to the boss or his designated employee, of course. They have the responsibility and dubious privilege of changing the pasture setup as necessary. The thing to remember, even when you don't agree or understand the reasons, is that the boss is a law unto himself and always has a good and valid reason for whatever he does! Always!

What most people who are not familiar with livestock don't know is that changing a gate can cause an awful lot of headaches for ranchers.

A gate that is shut when it should be open can separate cows from their calves causing the calves to go hungry and the cows to be uncomfortable with over-full udders, or it can keep cattle from water or grass.

On the other hand, leaving a gate open that should be closed causes just as much trouble. For starters, herds that are supposed to be separated, whether for breeding purposes or for grazing on certain pastures, will mix back together again.

It's time consuming, costly, and aggravating to have to repeat a week's work of weaning calves because someone left a gate open and the calves got back with their mamas.

It's especially bad if grade bulls are left free to mingle with registered cows. You can bet that, come calving time, there'll be some crossbred offspring among the purebred calves!

Sometimes fields have been planted and cattle shouldn't be in them until the grass or forage has come up and is growing well. Cows in those fields can ruin the grazing by their walking, feeding, or lying down.

Deer, who jump the fence or go under it, may do a lot of damage to a field, but a herd of cattle can really mess up the new growth when new grass is just emerging from the ground.

What happened when the gate to a pasture full of yearling bulls got left open one night? Twenty-four young bulls were investigating the countryside long before dawn arrived and the wide-open gate was discovered. Even though it was Sunday morning, we searched up and down the roads in the vicinity. By that afternoon, all of the bulls had been found roaming the highways and returned to their pasture, thankfully none the worse for their unscheduled day of adventure.

No harm was really done, except to the ego of the cowboy who had been guilty of leaving the gate open. In this case it was the boss who didn't close it. He had gone in the pasture to feed the bulls and had left it open until he came back out. Then, as cowboys do, he changed his mind, and continued on to a connecting pasture and out still another gate. After all that time, and with a lot on his mind, he simply forgot to return and close the first gate.

He received a lot of good-natured kidding which he accepted more or less in good spirit. All the rest of us gloatingly welcomed him with open arms to the ranks of us who have made mistakes. . .dumb and not so dumb. And, after all, we reasoned, everyone's entitled to *one* mistake, even the boss!

COUNTRY SOUNDS

The thing that almost all visitors to the country comment upon is, "It is so quiet out here. I just don't know how I would ever become used to the stillness."

I guess it *is* quiet.

Compared to the rumble of the city where there are cars and trucks constantly rumbling by, sirens screaming as they race through the streets, and the cacophony of noise that is generated by a multitude of people just living in a congested area, it must seem unnaturally silent in the country.

But we have our noises, too.

It's just that those of us who live the rural life tend to become more or less oblivious to the multitude of sounds around us.

Children shout in laughter, delight, or anger as they romp in play and call to each other or their pets.

Horses make a lot of noise as they gallop around and around a small pasture and whinny for others of their kind that are separated by a fence or two.

The quiet stillness is shattered by bulls bellowing loudly and threateningly as they push and shove and lock heads in an effort to establish their king-of-the-herd status.

Mama cows low mournfully for their calves after they are separated for weaning or sale.

Dogs bark hysterically at some nocturnal animal only they can see, or in answer to distant sounds only they can hear.

Cats squall, hiss, and spit furiously as they fight to stake their territory against some visiting feline romeo.

Squirrels chatter and chase each other around the yard in play, or scamper across the roof in quest of the pecans they can reach only by jumping into the tree from the nearby rooftop.

Armadillos, 'possums, and coons root around in the flower beds, even sometimes during the daylight hours, and noisily crunch the oak leaf mulch as they hunt for roots and tubers to eat.

Birds sing melodiously or nervously fuss at a cat they think might be threatening their young, and who very often is!

Geese, ducks, and other water fowl croak their messages to each other as they lift in flight from the pond behind the house. Even hummingbirds can be heard buzzing their tiny wings if one remains still and quiet enough for the miniature creatures to come near.

An alligator grunts at the edge of the pond and its young answer.

The still surface of the water is broken by the sudden splash of a fish as it feeds in the early morning haze or the late evening light.

A rain frog croaks loudly outside the window as the dawn breaks, begging for rain and pulling a sleeper reluctantly from the last few minutes of peaceful slumber.

Distant, alien sounds remind us of the outside world. An airplane drones or a helicopter clatters overhead, motor vehicles whiz by on the hard road a half-mile away and trains whistle hauntingly five miles in the distance

We do have our noises in the country. Sometimes we just have to be quiet and listen to them. It's a peaceful and natural sound, a sound country people take for granted but appreciate and love, nevertheless.

COW WORKIN' TIME

A hazy cloud of dust rises into the air and drifts lazily into the blue skies above a set of wooden cowpens nestled under a canopy of large oak trees. Suddenly, the stillness of the country solitude is shattered by the thunder of hooves and the lowing of hundreds of cattle.

It's cow working time on the Lazy J Bar Ranch!

Mounted cowboys, with their saddles creaking, swing their looped ropes around their heads or loudly pop their whips harmlessly in the air as they whoop at the herd of crossbred cows and calves to push it into the large wire holding pens.

It takes a lot of practice to learn the art of rounding up and penning cattle. Only experience can teach a cowboy where to position himself and his horse in order to keep the cattle moving and prevent them from cutting back to the woods or pasture from which they have just been rounded up.

Younger or inexperienced riders can be, and are, strategically placed to "plug a hole" when cattle are being moved, but it is the riders with the know-how who have the major responsibility in penning the cattle.

Once the herd is brought close to the pens a rider has to know when to hold his horse back and let the herd move on its own momentum. It's equally important to be able to sense the proper time to crowd the herd so they will enter the pens.

Cattle can be wary animals, especially when going through gates and entering pens. Most of the time, after they have been bunched up near an open gate, they will stand, or mill restlessly around the opening. The ones closest to it will look at it, sniff it, and just generally check it out!

Suddenly, as if seeing a light at the end of a tunnel and going toward it, one cow who is braver than the others, or maybe more curious, will slowly move up to the gate and gingerly make her way through it. A few others nearby will cautiously follow and the rush begins as they all play follow-the-leader through the gate. A few strays almost always cut back but are quickly rounded up and penned with the herd.

Once all of the cattle are inside the pen and the gate is closed they are given a few minutes to settle down. Mama cows who have been separated from their calves low, and their calves bleat, until they locate each other in the herd.

While the horses rest and water, the cowboys refresh themselves with a cold drink of water, tea, or coke. Then the hard, dirty work begins!

If the weather is dry, the work has to be done in the dust and the cowboys are soon covered with dirt and manure. If it has been raining, the pens will be muddy and the cowboys soon become coated with mud and manure. Sometimes they begin in dry pens and a sudden rainstorm turns the dirt into a quagmire, but the work goes on. Either way, they are one dirty, sweaty and smelly bunch before the day is done!

Mounted cowboys move slowly through the herd to cut a small number of animals into an adjoining pen. The rest of the work is done on foot as the cowboys move among the cattle or scramble along the fences.

All of the pens and chutes are constructed of heavy boards nailed onto large posts that are sunk deep into the ground to anchor them. As sturdy as they are, boards are frequently knocked down by the cattle and a hammer and nails are standard equipment at the pens.

The gates between the pens and along the chutes are hung so that they can be swung in either direction to make parting the cattle easier.

A metal squeeze chute is in place at the end of the parting chute. The sides can be adjusted to hold the animal securely in place while it is treated and then released to run free. This not only prevents the animal from hurting itself, the cowboy, or the veterinarian, it also takes less time to finish the job and lessens the stress on each animal.

In the past, until about the 1950's, cattle in Florida were put through a dipping vat. It was filled with water containing a solution to control ticks, grubs, lice, and flies. The cattle jumped from a chute into one end of the twenty-foot long vat, swam across it, and climbed steps at the other end to emerge dripping wet.

Today, they are sprayed in a pen using a gas-powered spray machine to wet them down thoroughly. All of the cattle are sprayed with the exception of the cull cows that are old or non-productive. These cows are parted into a smaller pen before the spraying is begun.

After being sprayed, the cattle are put through a parting chute where the calves are separated for weaning or whatever procedure is going to take place for them that day. The season of the year determines the work that will be done.

Working cattle in the Spring involves more procedures than in the Fall and takes longer. All animals are sprayed for external parasites except the cull cows. In addition, they all receive a dose of dewormer for internal parasites.

Wormers are available in three forms: injectable; paste, which is administered by mouth; and pour-on, which is poured on the animals back. Because resistance is built up against the dewormer by the parasites, we alternate the kinds of dewormers we use for greater efficiency.

Calves, like children, require regular medical attention in order to remain healthy. Instead of receiving inoculations as children do for smallpox, diphtheria, measles, whooping cough, tetanus, polio, or mumps, our calves are given a vaccination to protect them against eight different diseases. We value our animals and go to a great deal of expense and work to care for them properly.

Heifer calves are vaccinated against brucellosis and bull calves are neutered before returning to their mamas for the summer months.

Usually the cows are run through the chutes first and the calves are held up in a side pen to be worked later. Sometimes, if there's a really large bunch to be worked, the calves are kept in the holding area overnight and processed the next morning. When that happens the mama cows will hang around outside the pen and wait for their calves to be returned to them.

Dry cows are moved to a pasture where they are left to graze until they are marketed. Cows with calves are placed in pastures that are adjacent to rye fields for extra forage. This additional grass keeps the cows in good shape and helps the calves to grow big and strong.

In the Fall the cows are sprayed, dewormed, and blood samples are drawn to be checked for recertification as a brucellosis-free herd. The cows are also pregnancy checked by a veterinarian or one of the crew who has had training in the procedure.

Our livelihood depends on healthy productive cattle, and we cannot economically afford to keep a barren cow. If a cow is not bred, and it is her second year to be open, she is sold.

Replacement heifers are identified with the ranch mark and brand, the year, and their herd number to enable us to keep records on her calf production through the years. It's also a means of identifying her if she happens to stray or is "rustled." These heifers are placed in a pasture by themselves, fed through the winter, and wormed again in January or February. They have bulls with them and many calve when they are two years old. Since they are "first calf heifers," their calves are weaned from them at an earlier age than the older cows. After their calves are weaned, the heifers remain in a separate pasture until they join one of the main herds at three years of age.

Most steer calves have been marketed at an average weight of 525 pounds before cow working time in the Fall. Some go to the market but the majority of them are sold to an order buyer and shipped out in semi-trailer loads to a feed lot in another state. Before they are sold they receive a vaccination to protect them against sickness when they are mixed with other cattle in the feedlot.

They will be kept there and fed until they are approximately 1100 pounds before being processed for sale to consumers.

The steers that remain are too young or not bloomy enough to be sold with the main bunch. These calves, along with heifers that are not kept as replacement cows, are placed in our small feedlot and fed for a few months until they reach a good marketable size.

Whatever their destinations, all calves are wormed and weaned in the Fall before the new crop of calves starts coming.

The bulls are taken away from the cows at the end of July and returned to them in March, or as close to those dates as a busy ranch schedule allows. By controlling the breeding season, the calving season is also set and the majority of the cows drop their calves during the same time frame of November through March.

In addition to these major jobs of caring for our cattle, which can consume weeks of time, looking after their welfare is an on-going, year 'round job. A responsible rancher cares for his cattle and makes certain they have good grass for grazing, clean water available, and feed supplements such as protein blocks, molasses, and hay.

Our cows don't normally have trouble with their calving but occasionally something goes wrong and one will need help. Then we help her deliver her calf.

Experienced ranchers can take care of many of the medical problems of his cattle but he calls a veterinarian if a problem arises that is beyond his ability or expertise to handle. Our animals are watched for any that may need an extra worming or some other medical aid. A cow that is free of internal and external parasites, has adequate forage, and clean water is a healthier and more contented cow and this benefits her, her calf, and her owner.

A GOOD SAMARITAN

It was calving time and the newborn calves were busily frisking around their mamas and energetically digging in to eat after they had searched for, and found, the location of their meals on their mother's anatomy.

The phone rang about four o'clock in the afternoon and the caller identified herself as a teenage girl who lived a couple of miles away, in another county, to be exact.

After determining that we were, indeed, the Barthles who own the land by the county road "next to Mr. Whitehurst's," she proceeded to relate her story to me.

It seemed that some hours earlier the girl had been walking in our pasture. She didn't volunteer an explanation as to why she was there and at the moment it didn't occur to me to ask her.

She was a bit agitated as she told me how she had crossed an open field during her walk and had come across a cow and her newborn calf.

"The mother went off and left it," she exclaimed indignantly.

"Oh, no," I begged her silently. "Please don't say what I think you are going to say!"

I assured her that the cow most probably would return to her calf, but she insisted that there was something wrong with the cow.

"She would run a little way and fall down. Then she would get up, go a little further and fall down again," she explained.

Then she added what I didn't want to hear.

"The other cows crowded around the calf and knocked it down," she said.

I thought she was going to say that the calf was injured or dead so I was taken completely by surprise when she proudly stated, "So I picked it up and brought it home with me!" Home for her was a good two miles away!

Maybe it just seems that way, but when an unforeseen and difficult circumstance like this occurs, I am home by myself. Events that are only a nuisance to Joe and the boys assume emergency proportions to me. So it was on that day.

Joe was gone to a bull sale but Randy was around. I finally found him and informed him about our good Samaritan. Any rancher can readily relate to what *he* said.

Censored, it translated to "We don't need *that* kind of help!"

After going to her house in his pickup to retrieve the calf, Randy looked all over the open pasture for its mother but she was nowhere to be found.

Leaving the calf in the pasture, he went back to his barn to saddle a horse and ride back to search for the cow in the adjoining woods.

In the meantime, back at the house, Joe came home. His first action was to take some honey and water to the calf, which was his standard prescription whenever a calf needs some quick energy. The calf hadn't had a chance to nurse after birth and needed some nourishment *fast*. In fact, it sounded as if the cow probably hadn't even managed to finish the birthing process before the girl came along and scared her away.

After a long search through the woods Randy finally located the cow. Actually she was a two-year old, first-calf heifer and she wouldn't accept the calf. She just plain didn't want to have anything to do with it!

Occasionally a cow will refuse a calf for no apparent reason but in this case, there was probably no time for a bonding process and maybe she didn't recognize the calf as belonging to her.

It was a big calf, the heifer was a little on the small side and she'd had difficulty calving. That's no wonder, when she was disturbed right in the middle of it, but she was all right, or would be soon.

They took her to the pen at the feedlot, put her calf in with her, and hoped she would let it nurse eventually.

By the next morning nothing had changed. The cow and

the calf were still in the pen and the mother still refused to let her baby nurse. The temporary solution was to milk the cow and feed the calf with a bottle.

It took a long time that morning and evening and more effort during the next couple of days before the situation was put right and the cow would accept her baby and let it nurse. . . all because a well-meaning person who didn't know anything about cattle or ranching had tried to be helpful.

I never did see the girl. Neither did Joe, but he said she must have been pretty hefty and struggled hard to carry the calf so far.

"It got heavy for me, just carrying it to the pen," he said.

Bless her heart. She meant so well and only wanted to help but she sure caused a lot of trouble doing it.

I thought it sounded like something I might have attempted when I was a teenager, before I got involved in ranching. But I don't think I could have carried a calf, even a newborn one, two miles!

TREES, A HOLE, AND A HURRICANE

"But I want an oak tree lane," I insisted

I had seen a road with oaks planted on both sides and was impressed by the beauty of the lovely country road. I wanted one like it and had embarked on a campaign to have it!

Whenever there's a difference of opinion about a proposed project it sometimes seems that a man presents good, solid, and logical reasons to support his viewpoint against it while a woman can only muster up a vague, "I like it" or "because I think it will look nice."

Overall, given a choice, it seems that a man will usually opt for a practical course of action while a woman most often considers the beauty or attractiveness of the finished project. Maybe it's the word "finished" that scares him, because it probably mean lots and lots of work for him!

So it was with our oak tree lane.

Many years ago, when Jan was just a baby, I wanted to plant oak trees along both sides of the quarter-mile lane leading to the house. I admitted, reluctantly, that I knew it would require a lot of oak trees to be transplanted and watered until they "took hold." But I wanted it anyway, and after all, we do have an abundance of oak trees in the pastures!

Joe logically pointed out that if a hurricane blew some of the trees over we couldn't get to the hard road and would be stranded at our end of the lane. He conveniently overlooked the fact that a hurricane, or even a lot of rain, floods the road anyway!

Hurricanes usually come in twenty-year cycles in Florida and they were arriving more or less regularly at that time so I agreed that this was a valid point. I've never had much of an artistic talent but in my mind I kept picturing a canopy of green branches over the road that would make a beautiful approach to the house.

With little to lose, I did what any determined wife would do: I nagged a little, and begged a lot!

For the next few years we (he) planted and replanted, watered, and mowed, until the lane was more or less complete. A few trees have died but I don't have the nerve to ask for more to be planted. Anyway, the big trees have just about filled in the empty spaces where the others are missing.

The lane is beautiful and I enjoy driving and walking down it, especially in the spring and summer. We have a lot of dead limbs in the lane from the trees but so far none of them have blown over.

Not long after we got my oak tree lane growing, Joe's logic became active again. He noted that the pond behind the house would sometimes flood the barn, the yard, and even our laundry room after a lot of heavy rain. His solution to the problem was to excavate a deep hole at the edge of the pond and use the dirt to construct a bank that would help control the water. I didn't know it at the time, but he also had a hidden agenda: he wanted a dry spot out in the no-man's land between the barn, pond, and house where equipment that was not being used could be unhooked from the tractors.

I thought it would be unsightly and spoil the view of the pond. Nevertheless, the hole was dug, the bank was built, and the situation has been helped. Trailers, disks, mowers, and other equipment now occupy the dry area when they are idle.

Although I conceded the necessity for something to be done about the flooding, (after all it's great not to have to bale water out of the laundry room) I still think the view of the lake is not as pretty.

The years passed and then another hurricane came, a fairly mild one as hurricanes go. Hurricanes are named alphabetically and Keith, the eleventh one of the season, came roaring his way into the state.

Keith passed over Florida, dumping nearly seven inches of much-needed rain on our area. Here in the interior of Florida there was no major damage, just a few trees down, and a lot of Spanish Moss, leaves and twigs on the ground.

It's puzzling how one tree out of many in an area will fall while the others nearby remain standing. Perhaps it has something to do with their root system becoming loose in the saturated earth, or maybe an extra strong gust of wind catches one just right to push it over.

The wind was howling around the corners of the house that night, sounding like a freight train whistling as it approaches a crossing. The rain, coming down in torrents, was slammed against the windows in violent gusts. Being fatalists at heart, and knowing there was nothing we could do, we went to bed about midnight before the worst winds hit our area. Although we didn't know it, the damage to our house had already been done.

The next morning when we awoke all was peaceful, quiet and sunny with no heavy rains or high winds. There was still a light wind rustling the leaves and the skies were only partly cloudy as we ventured out to see what damage Keith had wrought.

As we expected, the yard was full of moss, twigs, leaves, and small limbs. The pond had risen until it was surrounding the house, and water was running through the culvert under the bridge on its way through the woods.

The big surprise was not seen until we reached the front yard and found a large limb that had broken and crashed onto the roof of the front sunporch.

Thinking back to the night before I remembered that I had been in the office at the back of the house, listening to the whistling of the wind and the crash of the rain. As I stood there I had heard a loud thump which, as nearly as I could tell, came from somewhere in the back yard.

I had turned on all of the outside lights and investigated but, not seeing anything that was a cause for alarm, we had gone to bed and slept soundly as Keith roared his way past.

We decided that the noise I had heard was the limb landing on the roof, but it wasn't visible from inside the house. The roof had suffered only minor damage because the limb was still partially attached to the tree and had fallen across another big branch that kept the full weight off the roof.

We had to hire a tree service to remove the two very large limbs but as "they" say, "It's an ill wind that blows no good," even hurricane winds.

Just weeks before we had discussed trimming the big branches back from the roof. Now from necessity it was done and a bonus was that we had a large supply of wood for the fireplace and a big pile of wood chips for mulching the flower beds.

The biggest bonus for me was one for which I had waited many years!

Joe's mother, a lovely and pleasant lady, had planted two trees in front of the house before we were married. There was also one out by the barn which Joe had planted to shade Dude's lot. Dude was our stallion and our favorite horse.

That tree had blown over and fallen across the fence and lot. That morning Joe couldn't find Dude in his stall, nor anywhere in his lot. There were a few anxious moments as we imagined him dead under the tree. It was both comical and a relief to find him standing placidly under the shelter of the branches lying across the fences, just high enough off the ground for him to walk and stand under!

After all the years I had waited, I was finally able to say, "See, it wasn't the trees I wanted planted that caused the trouble."

And we laughed together about it because while it was close, it wasn't exactly an "I told you so!"

A GAME OF PEEKABOO

I didn't really feel like walking that day, certainly not the brisk walking decreed by my doctor. It wasn't as much a physical thing as just a mental laziness. However, I finally put my walking shoes on and set out to take a leisurely stroll. I hoped I could surprise some deer grazing on an open field. Even though I've lived in the country most of my life I've not had, nor taken, the opportunity to get out in the woods much, so every adventure I have involving animals is new and exciting to me.

Taking my rod and reel, I walked through the barn and made a detour along the edge of the pond to try my luck at catching a fish. The surface of the sparkling blue water was still and quiet, with no fish feeding. Only the sound of birds as they circled overhead and the distant bellowing of bulls broke the quietness of the Sunday afternoon.

After casting a few times and deciding it was too early in the afternoon for the fish to bite, I left my tackle leaning up against a spreading oak tree and continued on through the horse pasture to the woods.

The horses, who are turned out of the barn to graze during the day when they are not being ridden, came up to me to sniff with curiosity before whirling with a snort to run away.

As I skirted the scrub about a half-mile from the house I spied an animal under the trees in the distance. I thought it was either a small dog, a coon, or an armadillo, but I couldn't make out which. Having a curious nature, I wanted to get a closer look so I began angling towards it, trying to remember and practice all I had ever read about walking stealthily and quietly, like a hunter or an Indian.

I soon found out that it's not an easy feat for a novice to walk through the woods quietly! Leaves and small twigs seem to explode with sound, even when stepped on very cautiously. Nevertheless, I went slowly on, carefully placing one foot in front of the other as I peered at the ground, choosing spots to step that were relatively clear of twigs, growing cover. . .and snakes!

As I got closer to the animal I recognized that it was a coon so engrossed in rooting in the ground for roots or grubs, or whatever coons eat, that it didn't see me until our paths of travel had almost intercepted.

Finally, when we were about twenty feet apart he suddenly spied me and quickly scampered for safety in the nearest refuge, a large oak tree which was ten feet away.

Once safely ensconced there he began a game of peekaboo, with him doing all the peeking at me from the back side of the tree trunk where he apparently considered himself to be out of sight and therefore safe.

He would move from one side of the trunk to the other, each time peeking out at me before ducking back to move to the other side where he ventured another look to see if the alien creature he feared was still standing there

This routine was repeated for seven or eight times as I stood there enjoying the sight of the tiny little face with the inquisitive white-circled eyes that was both amusing and captivating.

Finally, he either didn't see me or had decided I was not a danger to him and he gathered up enough courage to venture around to my side of the tree. Once there, he crawled up and down and back and forth on the trunk in that location for a while.

I had been standing motionless right out in the open, scarcely daring to breathe or swallow for fear of scaring him away. At last, gathering his remaining courage, he crawled to the ground and stood at the base of the tree where I was able to get a really good look at him.

By then I had decided to wait him out and see what his next move would be. I knew that his instinct warned him that something wasn't quite right, but he couldn't seem to figure out just what the problem was.

For the next five minutes my little friend remained close to the base of the tree, every little while lifting his nose high into the air as he attempted to smell the unseen danger which he so obviously sensed was near.

From time to time he would even rise up on his hind legs to sniff the air. But it was a still, hot day with not even a hint of a breeze, and he apparently couldn't get my scent, even though I was standing just twenty feet away!

The blackberry bushes under the tree tempted him and eventually he began moving from one of them to another, seeking the juicy black fruit.

All the time he was unaware that he was edging closer to me as I stood quietly. Suddenly, at about fifteen feet's distance, he spied me and loped back to the tree to begin his favorite game again!

This time the rules seemed to be different. Each time he peeked out from behind the trunk of the tree he did so from a position higher up in the tree. The last glimpse I caught of him was when he was fifty feet up into the branches and still climbing!

Actually I was kind of glad the game was over because, while it was enjoyable, he was getting all of the action and I was becoming stiff and tired from standing as motionless as a statue!

I continued my walk in search of the deer, which weren't in the field, and when I came back there wasn't any sign of friend Coon either. I didn't know if he was still hiding in the branches or had taken advantage of my absence to escape but it was fun while it lasted!

As I made my way back through the pasture a bunch of heifers spied me and came trotting over, probably with the hope of getting some mineral pellets although they are usually fed from a truck, or more likely were just curious. Just before they reached me they started running and split into two groups on either side to go around me. After regrouping they whirled and thundered away, back to the other end of the pasture.

I continued on and reached the pond again as the sun was just beginning to sink behind the trees and the western sky was filling with the rosy colors of approaching twilight.

Retrieving my fishing tackle I decided to give the fish another opportunity at my bait before the mosquitoes drove me inside. This time I had more luck. I landed a bass that I estimated to weight about three-fourths of a pound—not a keeper, so I released it to grow some more.

Suddenly something really big made a whirl, grabbed my bait and snapped my line. I had been watching a small gator for a few days so I thought it might have been him.

At any rate, I didn't have any more bait with me, night had fallen, and the mosquitoes were beginning to drone and attack. I ambled on to the house, content and at ease at the end of another beautiful day in the country.

THE BEST OF TWO WORLDS

The storm had appeared suddenly, as Florida storms so often do. Where only minutes before the skies had been filled with sunshine and fluffy white clouds, it was now almost dark as great banks of black clouds moved into the area.

I walked the floor as the lightning flashed and crackled in the sky, thunder rolled with a deafening roar, rain came down in torrents, and the frenzied wind lashed the limbs of trees and shrubs into myriad freakish shapes in a furor of movement.

It was one of the cow working days and I was home all alone. Since I knew there was shelter at the cowpens I wasn't concerned for the safety of the family. I was worried about Dude, who was grazing in the pasture behind the house. I knew the rain wouldn't hurt him but the lightning was popping and striking everywhere. He was valuable to us and if he were killed by lightning, not only would our favorite horse be gone, but we would lose a valuable asset as well.

About that time Mark came by and I asked him to catch Dude and put him in the barn. Normally Dude would come running to be haltered when he was called but today was different.

Mark tried. He called and called, but Dude wouldn't come. Mark tried to walk up to him to put the halter on him but Dude wasn't having any of that either. He was so excited and scared by the storm that all he wanted to do was to run around and around the field in a frenzied state.

Finally I called to Mark and told him to let it go. If Dude was going to be struck by lightning we couldn't help it. I sure didn't want Mark to be a victim as well.

For the duration of the storm, I alternated between walking the floor and peering out the windows to see if Dude was still on his feet. And I began comparing the experiences of nature which country folk have with those of people who live in the cities and towns.

Only those who have seen it can appreciate the fresh

sparkling beauty of a world that has been washed clean by rain when the awful majesty of a storm or a gentle rain shower has passed.

People who have lived in cities all their lives, surrounded by buildings, can't welcome a rising sun as its warm rays dispel the darkness of the night or wash away the fog that shrouds the world in a mysterious haze.

Nor have they seen the blazing yellow ball of a setting sun as it slowly sinks behind the green fields and woods and fills the sky with vivid colors until it darkens enough for the twinkling stars to emerge and dot the vast expanse of the heavens with spots of light

They've never experienced the awesome beauty of a night sky which is dominated by a full golden moon radiating almost enough light to illuminate the printed word. No one who hasn't seen the sight can fully imagine the fresh untouched beauty of a winter morning when fields are blanketed with a fresh white frost, icicles hang like needles from dripping faucets and puddles of water are covered with a shining film of ice.

The imagination cannot conjure up the glory of a hot summer morning when dew shines on the grass like diamonds and the footprints of human or animal leave a wandering trail across the pristine beauty.

Nor is it possible, without having experienced the breeze as it ripples the leaves in a shade tree, to imagine the refreshing coolness as it gently wafts away the heat.

Those who have only hot pavement or a city park in which to walk cannot imagine the peacefulness of a quiet stroll through the cool green woods and the breathtaking excitement of watching birds and animals as they play or forage for food in their natural habitat.

Having never heard anything but the sound of cities, how could they know about the contentment one experiences while sitting in the dark and watching fireflies twinkle as whippoorwills, owls, frogs, and crickets break the stillness of the night with their songs?

City folks cannot know the joy of witnessing a deer in flight, with its white tail flagging its defiance, and the gracefulness of its leap over a fence or fallen log.

While they may have seen photographs of our national bird, they have never felt the thrill of seeing the American Bald Eagle soaring gracefully through the skies or perching majestically in a tree as it surveys its kingdom.

All of these thoughts went through my mind as the storm raged around the house. I know that those of us who live in the country may sometimes find it inconvenient to live far from town, but I think that most of us will agree that we've got the best of two worlds.

As the storm abated and finally dried away, I was relieved to look out and see Dude placidly grazing in his pasture. He had survived the storm and had settled down to the important business of feeding himself!

RANCH PETS

Every ranch has a dog, or dogs. Besides helping pen cows, dogs are good for a lot of things, not the least of which is to bark at 'possums, coons, armadillos, and other dogs in the middle of the night. They don't always catch, or even chase, anything. They just bark. . . and bark. . .and bark. To add to our frustration, the dogs usually stand just outside the window where we human inhabitants of the ranch are attempting to sleep.

The red fox is a native to Florida as well as to a number of other states. It is an animal that looks much like a small dog except that his ears are larger, triangular, and furrier than a dog's. His snout is more pointed and his jaws are straighter. One of his characteristics is his long bushy tail. Fox like to prowl at night and eat rabbits, ground birds, poultry, rats, mice, frogs, worms, beetles and fruit.

The fox has a yelping bark. If captured, he will sometimes pretend to be dead, much like a 'possum, but will run away as soon as he is freed. Some people enjoy a fox hunt more than any other kind of hunt. The fox is not killed or captured; the hounds just chase it and bring it to bay. They do just what the name implies: they "hunt" it.

The fun for the owners of the dogs lies in listening to the dogs bark, yap, and bay as they trail the fox through the woods, across the pastures, and along the lakes or streams. They enjoy identifying the "voice" of their dog in the chorus of the pack as it trails the fox. When the fox is "treed" or "goes to ground" in a hole, the dogs are gathered up and taken home. The fox is left free to lead the dogs on another merry chase some other night.

One night we were invited to a fox hunt. We declined the invitation and retired to bed, but not, as it turned out, to sleep. In the distance we could hear the dogs and follow the hunt as it progressed. Closer and closer the pack of baying dogs came, in full chase of the fox. As they raced, barking, through our yard and right by our bedroom window, I was rooting for the fox!

Sometimes, after a fox hunt, a dog will be lost. It may become separated from the pack and can't be found when it's time to load in the truck and return home. Quite often we have had dogs or owners turn up at our house the next day, looking for each other. The dogs usually have collars with a name and telephone number of the owner, and we are able to reunite them.

Over the years we've had quite a turnover in dogs. Here I'm referring to stock dogs, not your run-of-the-mill pets, although they served that purpose too. The kids loved to rope the dogs and, before they got too big and heavy, they thought it was great fun to ride them.

One big white and brown cur dog named Blondie agreeably allowed himself to be ridden over and over again. The kids would get astride his back, and Blondie would take a few steps before the rider would tumble to the ground. When Blondie got tired, he didn't get snappish; he would just trot off, usually dragging a protesting kid determined to remount for another ride.

Blondie would duck under a low-lying pickup truck or trailer and remain there until he got his rest. When he felt like playing again, he would emerge and continue the game.

Only once did Blondie show his temper. Randy was about four or five years old and was throwing sand at Blondie while the hungry dog was eating. Although he probably did not mean to bite the kid, he snapped at him and, unluckily, bit him just over the eye in the eyebrow area. It wasn't a serious bite, but the great amount of blood that ran down past Randy's eye and over his face sure scared one young mother!

The dogs at our place seemed to have a high mortality rate; only a few have lived to a ripe old dog's age. The leading causes of death were injuries caused from being run over or snakebites.

Stock dogs lead a pretty hard working life sometimes. Mostly though, they just eat, sleep and bark at strangers. On

the long cattle drives, racing back and forth, they help to keep the cattle bunched and moving in the right direction. There, and in the cattle pens, they get a lot of kicks and stompings from the cattle. Those who are not victims of accidental death are prone to wear out at an earlier age than dogs who are only pets. As most ranchers do, we take good care of our dogs, but they have occupational hazards just the same as cowboys.

Cats are also part of country living. Although their duties are not as obvious and rigorous as those of dogs, cats have the important job of keeping the rat population under control in the barns and feed bins.

At our house the principal occupation of the cats during the day would seem to be sleeping near the back door. That location makes it convenient for them to wake and meow pitifully whenever the door is opened. As many times as they have been put out, they should know that they're not allowed inside, but they like to dart in the open door every chance they have.

Cats around here have lost their lives mostly from hiding in car engines, or being run over, or from being caught by the dogs.

One cat who was especially bright devised his own plan for evading death by the dogs. Before venturing into the hazardous war zone between house and barn, Tom would stand very still and scout the area for dogs. When he was satisfied that all was safe, he would streak for the barn at top speed and scamper up the ladder into the safety of the hayloft.

Once there, he would stand in the open doorway as if he were taunting the dogs and saying, "I fooled you this time." He would brave the danger again and repeat the exercise later on the return trip to the house.

Sometimes Tom would misjudge the situation and almost get caught. The dogs' barking and Tom's squalling while he tried to outrun them would bring us many times to the back door as we tried to halt the chase.

Many people who live in cities and wish, for one reason or another, to rid themselves of their pets, bring them to the country and turn them loose. If someone doesn't adopt them, they are likely to starve.

But some do survive, especially the dogs. They band together in packs and roam the woods and countryside, living off the wildlife they are able to kill. Sometimes a band will get really ferocious and kill calves, and not always just to eat.

Country people aren't able to adopt and feed all of the animals that are dumped on them. It's too bad people don't realize how much better off the animals would be if they were taken to an animal shelter for adoption or to be put to sleep.

Many of our cats have been drop-offs and some of them have been beautiful animals. One in particular was a lovely gray who seemed to have some Persian blood. She had been neutered and obviously had been a house cat. At first we called her Thomas but later changed it to Thomasina when we got to know her better.

One who adopted us wasn't beautiful; she wasn't even pretty! She had to be the ugliest cat any of us had ever laid eyes on! She was a skinny black, yellow, brown and gray calico with a long, skinny tail. Because she looked so much like a 'possum, we called her "Pogo."

Still, she showed promise. She ate a lot, was loving and gentle, and meowed really well. One day she half-killed a small black snake while just playing with it in the yard. It wasn't clear to us if she tried to worry it to death or scared it out of its senses with her ugliness. Anyway, the snake was rescued and returned to freedom in the woods.

Pogo disappeared one day while we were gone on a short trip. We knew it wasn't because of hunger because one of our sons was feeding her. Finally, we concluded that some one came along and took her as a curio. There's not that many cats who are so outstandingly ugly!

Al, short for *Ag Libs*, the name of a weekly column I was writing when she appeared, is another calico cat but of softer shades and really quite pretty. Al surprised us with a litter of kittens. Of all the cats in our experience, she had the strangest way of mothering her babies.

The five kittens were born in the hayloft and the very first thing one did was fall over the edge and down into a horse stall where it was stepped on. Joe put the other four in a box so they couldn't scoot over the edge and fall to their deaths, too.

Al promptly removed them. Then, one by one, they disappeared until we thought they were all dead. One theory was that the big rats in the barn ate them. Another was that Al brought them down and Britta, Mark's big black Rottweiler, ate them. They would have been a mere appetizer for her!

Al spent her time roaming around the barn and yard but there was no sign of her kittens. Suddenly two of them reappeared in a corner just inside the barn door. Later in the evening Joe heard a kitten meowing in the little pasture behind the house. He could hear it but he couldn't find where it was hidden. Finally, after searching for quite a while he located it inside a piece of tin he had wrapped around the trunk of a pecan tree in a vain effort to keep the squirrels out of the tree.

That made three recovered kittens and only one still missing! When the fourth one turned up in the barn with the others the next day, we were expecting it.

It's pretty common knowledge that mother cats are likely to move and hide their kittens but we never heard of one who put each one in a different spot, and then returned them before their eyes were open!

Maybe with her animal instinct Al knew that she was near death and wanted us to care for her babies because after they were all back together she became desperately sick with what I assumed was "kitten birth fever." Whatever she had must have made her sterile because she's never produced another litter.

Although the kittens were awfully young, we were able to save them all by hand feeding them.

After Al had recuperated and her babies were about half grown, we were all outside one afternoon telling Kathy and her family good-bye one day.

Britta, who must have thought a kitten, even a half-grown one, would be just about right for a snack, sneaked in and grabbed one. All at once the peaceful scene disintegrated. Britta was growling, the kitten was squalling, Al was screeching and Nick was screaming!

Here is the scene: a two-car carport, with cars in place.

Here are the characters: Al was on one side of the carport and Britta was mouthing the kitten on the other side, with the two cars in between. Nick, age nine, and I were in front of the cars, between Britta and Al.

Al quickly went on the attack to save her offspring. At the same instant that she launched herself through the air in front of the cars, Nick, unaware of what was happening, stepped into her path. Al slammed into him and her teeth sank into his backside!

She didn't even hesitate but continued on and lit into Britta, who dropped the kitten to defend herself against the howling demon who was attacking.

The scene dissolved into pandemonium: one little boy screaming in terror and pain and holding his rear end, a five-pound cat mixing it up with an eighty-five pound dog with all the sound effects that go with a cat and dog fight, and five adults and four other kids trying to find out what was wrong with Nick and attempting to break up the fight.

I, being the closest to Nick, was the only one to see what had happened. And the only one to see Al on the attack. With her teeth and claws bared and her hair standing on end, she was a perfect model for a cartoon of a mad cat!

Mark reacted by grabbing Britta. Britta dropped the kitten, who promptly scampered under the nearest car to safety and was no worse for the attack except for a coat which was wet from Britta's slobbering jaws.

Al retreated and was serenely washing her kitten under the car, Nick was still crying, though more quietly, and Jan was anxiously trying to find out why her son was crying. Through my laughter I attempted to explain while I pulled Nick's pants down to discover the extent of the damage to his posterior.

The two neat puncture wounds on his seat resembled a snake bite and were just barely oozing blood. After things quieted down we continued our good-byes to the Paiges and Mark went home with Britta. Nick's wound was cleaned and Jan checked with the doctor about the advisability of a tetanus shot. In no time at all Nick was out playing, and except for a little soreness he was fine the next day.

Cats and dogs have never resided in our house. The King of the Castle wouldn't allow it! But that doesn't mean we didn't have our share of animals inside anyway. The kids saw to that.

We had rabbits, 'possums, coons, and squirrels in boxes. They were all babies, and all motherless, I was solemnly assured by earnest little voices.

We also had snakes, frogs, butterflies, crickets, and the like in jars, fish and turtles in bowls, and hamsters, chicks, gerbils, and birds in cages. . .not all at the same time, thank goodness!

Once we even had a litter of newborn pigs in the kitchen during freezing weather which we tried desperately, and most unsuccessfully, to keep warm, feed with a syringe, and save their lives.

Actually, they were Mark's hogs but since he was busy showing his steer at the county fair, it's an easy guess who most of the job fell to.

Kathy was a very naive little girl, a lot like her Mom, and

believed most anything she was told. She had a small turtle, about the size of a silver dollar, in a bowl and loved to feed it.

"Kathy," I told her, "If you don't quit feeding that turtle so much it is going to get too big."

One day Joe found a turtle that was at least six inches long and four inches wide. He removed the little turtle from the bowl and replaced it with the big one while Kathy was at school.

As she usually did when she arrived home from school Kathy went immediately to feed her turtle. I stood back and waited for her reaction, which wasn't long in coming and was not in the least what we had expected!

She let out the loudest, heartbroken cry and said, "You told me not to feed it so much!"

Even though I was laughing so hard, I had to gather her in my arms and comfort her while I explained the trick her Daddy had played on her.

The kids really enjoyed their assortment of pets over the years. If we could have gathered all of them from over the years into one menagerie we could have probably charged poor little city younguns to look at them. City folks just don't have the joys that we country folk do!

A HUNTING EXPERIENCE

Each fall brings the "great migration" of a large segment of the male population as well as quite a number of the opposite sex. It seems that the only requirement for joining in is to be old enough or big enough to carry the required equipment: bow and arrows, muzzle loader, shotgun, canvas chair, and so forth.

It's hunting season! During the next two to three months hunters will spent every weekend and a lot of weekdays in the woods.

Those who are uninitiated can only imagine the joy to be experienced in rising and trekking to the woods while it's still dark, to sit quietly and listen to the night sounds, and wait for daylight to arrive. The hope and expectation of getting a shot at the "big one", or "any one" with horns, probably makes the hunters impervious to the numbing cold.

Most hunters are even happy to get one without horns during doe season when doe permits are issued because there are more deer in an area than there's forage for them. It's a lot more humane to harvest the overpopulation for food than to leave them to die from disease or starvation.

Shooting at ducks as they whiz across the range of vision while taking off or landing on the water apparently is a wonderful and stimulating experience. Personally, I can't imagine anything that could equal the fun of wading into the brisk cold pond to retrieve the birds that have fallen there!

Dove shoots? Imagine the excitement of shooting box after box of shells at the erratically flying birds. . .and coming home with hearing diminished and somewhat less than the legal limit of a very expensive meal!

Then take wild hogs. They're a real challenge to the hunter because they're potentially dangerous. At least, they're probably the most ferocious game in our area, and, undoubtedly, the ugliest! They have a nuisance value, too, since they like to root up pastures in search of food.

Quail hunting sounds to be the least exciting kind of hunting. The hunter waits for the dog to point the covey. The hunter flushes them and shoots. Next comes the fun part. The hunter then searches for the fallen birds which the dog can't or won't retrieve. Quail can also be the main course of a very expensive meal!

The amazing thing is that the same people who have to be practically hoisted out of bed most of the year can actually set their own alarm clocks and spring out of bed unassisted during hunting season!

As you have probably guessed, I've been writing with tongue in cheek, but the truth is I've never been a hunter. Neither has Joe which probably explains my lack of interest. I've never had the desire to shoot anything, especially a deer that is blessed with such big brown eyes. It seems that just about all wildlife have dark eyes.

I think I caught the fever from our sons, who are all avid and competent hunters as well as dedicated conservationists. Maybe it was just for a new experience, or it could have been because I missed the trophies that used to hang in our family room and which were removed to their new locations when each of the boys were married.

Whatever the reason, I got an unexpected yen to shoot a deer. . .but not just any deer. Since I never expected to harvest more than one, I wanted it to be a big buck with a trophy rack. I wanted to have it mounted to fill the empty space on the wall.

Mark offered to take me hunting but on the day we were scheduled to go it was cold and windy and I had a bad cold. He went by himself and reported later that he sat and watched a big bunch of deer for a long time.

"I didn't shoot, though," he told me proudly. "I was saving them for you."

The next afternoon was a warm day with the sun shining brightly and banks of white clouds drifting lazily overhead. When Mark arrived for me he said, "Mom, even if you don't shoot anything, you'll have a good time just watching the deer."

I didn't have the regulation camouflage outfit which Mark wore so I had dressed in the most drab, colorless clothes in my wardrobe. I felt sort of like a little brown chipmunk in my brown pants, sweater, and moccasins. I considered splashing some green paint on to make something that resembled an official cammo suit but decided against that!

Mark gave me a quick lesson in sighting the gun and showed me where and how to aim and shoot it. He also emphasized how important it is to be still when hunting.

"Be absolutely motionless," he cautioned.

He was so insistent on that point that I began to get the impression that it might be more important to stay still than to be able to shoot. I found out why later.

We drove to the woods in his jeep and after hiking through more woods and crawling under a fence, we sat down under a big shady oak tree by a water hole at the edge of the oak scrub. . .near the "Enchanted Forest."

This was exactly the same spot where Mark had sat and watched so many deer the day before. He told me, and I believed him, that the deer would probably be back that day.

I'm not very tall, only five feet, one and a half inches, and not real hefty. The rifle he gave me was so big and so heavy that I couldn't even begin to hold it steady.

My next instruction from Mark was, "Pull your knees up and rest the gun on them to steady it."

I've always had the comforting knowledge that my legs, though not real long, were adequate in length. They do, after all, reach from my hips to the ground. I soon discovered that they weren't long enough to reach high enough for me to steady that monstrosity of a gun in a position where I could look through the scope.

My patient son said, "I don't think you ought to try to shoot anything today. We'll just watch the deer, and borrow a lighter gun for you another time."

He said that just before he placed the gun across my legs, handed me the binoculars, told me again to be VERY STILL as I watched for deer, and went to sleep! I wasn't real sure how

I was going to balance the gun, look through the binoculars, and stay motionless all at the same time. Nevertheless I tried and thought I succeeded very well. . .for a beginner.

For the next hour or so Mark slept and I diligently alternated scanning the edge of the oak scrub and the open rye field for deer. . .any deer!

The only moving things that came within my sight were cows, robins and one beautiful fox squirrel who paraded right in front of us to reach a nearby tree. As instructed, I was being VERY STILL!

Just at dark when Mark roused I thanked him for the enjoyment I had received from watching all of the deer. I didn't think he was the only one who had been patient that day so in my sweetest mother's voice I noted, "I've seen more wildlife while sitting on my front porch than I have seen today."

I also thought, but didn't say, that taking your mother hunting and making sure she sat quietly for a couple of hours was a very good way to escape two very active babies and get a much needed nap!

I was accused of being a jinx and keeping the deer away. That might be a possibility since everybody else in the family reported seeing herds of up to sixty deer grazing on an open pasture. Not me. Never. All I ever glimpsed were a few white tails flagging as the animals race away through the woods.

"How's your fishing?" Mark asked me.

I had to admit that I have never caught a big bass. Just little ones, and some brim, perch, and catfish.

"I kinda think maybe we ought to work on getting you a big fish before we aim for a big buck," he teased me.

At least I thought he was teasing but he's never taken me hunting again, nor fishing.

The episode has a sequel. A few days later the same son returned to the same spot, sat under the same tree, and shot a twelve point buck. . .a beautiful trophy.

I thought, and said, that it was just as well I was not with him that day 'cause he probably wouldn't have let me shoot it anyway. Although he insisted he would have, I'm not sure that he wouldn't have wanted that trophy for himself.

Anyway, even if I could have managed to put the binoculars down and raise the gun, I probably would have missed the deer!

A TIME OF HOPE

Unlike fairs in the northern areas of the country, fairs in Florida are held during the winter months. Because it isn't as hot and rainy at that time of the year, attendance is better and the fairs are able to attract more interesting events.

Homemakers produce their best needlework, crafts, and culinary triumphs for display and judging.

School exhibit buildings are filled with students' best work. They proudly display samples of what they have learned and accomplished, and anxiously inquire of parents and grandparents, "Did you see mine? Did you see mine?"

Friendly competition exists between community and civic clubs as they decorate booths to exhibit the handiwork and hobbies of their residents or projects of their organization.

Cattle, horses, rabbits, chickens, goats, swine and other animals are on display. They are all judged and all receive a ribbon of some color.

Pet shows are a popular part of the fair and so is the wildlife exhibit. Farm machinery, cars, boats, and recreation vehicles are on display and draw their share of interested observers.

Baby pageants are popular although the parents and relatives are often more concerned with the results of the judging than are the participants. Many of the little contestants appear to wish they were anywhere else except on that stage!

When our older children were small I entered them in the baby shows. At the time, their Daddy didn't object. However, when five year old Larry was crowned the Prince of Pasco County, that was the end of it. During the next year Joe had to take too many days off from his work to view parades all over the county where Larry was required to participate!

The biggest drawing card at our county fair is usually the queen contest. A bevy of belles demonstrate their talents and beauty for the judges and the audience, and hope for the coveted title of "Miss Pasco County."

At various times Jan, Kathy, and Beth represented Pasco County Cattlemen's Association in this and in the Florida Cattlemen's Sweetheart competition held each year at the state convention.

For the children and young of age or heart, the midway is the fair. Here cotton candy, caramel apples, popcorn, foot-long hotdogs, ice cream, french fried potatoes and onions, elephant ears, polish sausage, and a myriad of other tummy twisters are consumed, much of which is promptly lost after a turn on one of the wild rides!

Food booths operated by local groups are strategically located around the grounds and offer everything from strawberry shortcake to spaghetti, chicken pileau, barbecue, hamburgers, and steak.

Entertainment is non-stop and both educational and commercial demonstrations are staged.

The spots that have always meant Fair Week to us were the show barn and sale arena. That's where we almost lived for the duration of the fair. Except for the feeding that is a must during the winter, work on the ranch quite literally stopped for five days.

Of course there was the mandatory visit to the school and 4-H exhibit buildings, but for many years about the only things I ever saw at the fair were the three "B's:" the barn, the Cattlemen and CattleWomen's food booth, and the bathroom!

Our children were steer exhibitors, as many as five in one show! Their projects began in early September when they acquired their steers. They then had to finish them out by fair time in February. From September on it was a lot of hard work while they learned the responsibility of caring for their animals and keeping accurate records.

The tension mounted as the time to take the steers to the fair neared. It culminated on the weekend before, when they had to transfer the records they had kept to a new, clean record book and write down the stories about their problems, successes, and learning experiences.

Just about every year we would discover on the Saturday or Sunday that we hadn't taken photos of the exhibitor and his or her finished steer. Many times we took pictures on Sunday, I had them developed on Monday, and they would be in the record books when the children turned them in on Monday night at the weigh-in.

"I'm not doing this next year," I would say. "You are going to have to learn to remember these things."

But when the next time came, who did it? Good ole Mom! After all, what are Moms for? You can't let your kids down! I probably should have reminded them earlier, and I would have, if it hadn't slipped my mind, too.

On show night there was always an air of excitement which pervaded the barn. Strolling along the aisles you could feel the tension as youngsters worked under their parents' and club leaders' guidance to have their animals groomed "just right" for judging.

In those days the steers' tails were teased and fluffed, not balled in a net as they are now, and there were no top knots left on the heads. The children washed the steers on the day of the show, rather than on the day before as they do now, so show day was a busy time.

The appearance of the boys and girls was most important. It was always impressive when they came into the show ring, neatly dressed and proudly wearing their 4-H or FFA jackets, leading their immaculately groomed steers to be judged.

Kathy, who was small for her age, showed her first steer when she was eight. We always laugh when we think of that tiny little girl leading her big steer around the ring, tugging to keep him moving, and jerking on his halter to keep him under control.

Our kids didn't cry when their animals were sold. It was partly because, living on a ranch, they knew the steer had been raised for food. They freely admitted, too, that they were tired of him: tired of feeding, brushing, and leading him every day; tired of being kicked, stomped, and dragged around as they worked with him and taught him to lead. Right then, nothing looked better to them than the prospect of a few months of freedom before they chose their new steer for the next year.

They did cry the few times when a steer didn't make it into the show. That does happen sometimes when an animal doesn't reach his potential or won't gentle down, no matter how much care is lavished on him.

It's a big disappointment for a youngster to work for months with a steer and then, for one reason or another not make it into the show. Hard as it is for the youngster, though, they learn from the experience that everything in life doesn't always work out right. It's a valuable lesson in putting disappointments behind and going on to the next project. Although it's not one we would choose for our children, it's a good thing for them to know and carry on into their adult life.

Now the grandchildren are showing steers, hogs, and heifers. It's great for us just to be there and cheer them on. . .with no responsibility!

OUR OWN PARADE

The second most exciting thing about the county fair for the kids, after the steer show and sale, was the opening day parade. For more years than I care to remember our family was involved with it, or more accurately, in it up to our necks it seemed sometimes.

Joe and the kids rode their horses in the parade each year and that was a big production for both of us! He had what I thought was the comparatively easy job of saddling and hauling mounts to town; riding in the parade with the kids; and unsaddling, loading, and hauling the horses home.

My assigned role was to load the car with the clothes the kids were to wear in the parade, pick them up at school, help them change from their school uniforms, and deliver them to their designated spot in the lineup where Joe was waiting with the horses. From there I hurried to a vantage point with the little ones who were too young to ride. We would watch for the family and wave as they rode by, take pictures, and then scurry back with the car to pick them up when they had dismounted.

The kids, at least, have fond memories of the times when they "rode in the parade." The horses all behaved reasonably well, the kids were all pretty good riders, and nobody ever got hurt.

My most vivid recollection of parade incidents is one which occurred the year I made matching western shirts for Joe, Randy, Jan, and Steve. I was real proud of those green shirts. They even had pearl snap buttons and I thought how nice my mounted group would look as they rode along and waved at the crowd.

Randy, at eight, was the oldest and was riding by himself on Missy. Officially, she was my golden palomino mare but by that time I never rode her any more. She was gentle, not too big and was more or less Randy's horse at the time. As the kids grew, though, and graduated to a bigger horse, the one behind in age would inherit her.

Jan was on her black and white "Paint" pony who was half Tennessee Walking Horse and half Shetland Pony. We had bought him for her when he was two. She was three and he had promptly bucked her off . . . luckily in some soft sand. After that he had settled down, but just to be safe, Joe had him on a lead rope for the parade.

Steve, who was only three, rode in the saddle in front of his Daddy who was riding a bay gelding.

The parade was led off by dignitaries of the county and were followed by civic and business floats, marching bands, walking members of various organizations both children and adults, and towards the end the fire engines, tractors, and agricultural equipment.

The mounted groups were placed at the very end, for obvious reasons!

Kathy and Larry enjoyed the clowns who were selling balloons and other parade momentos and were intrigued by the miniature cars and motorcycles as they did "wheelies" and "doughnuts" in and around the parade units.

The parade went by and we watched it—to the very end—but no Barthles came by.

Finally, when the cleaners came to sweep the street after the horses had passed, and there was still no sign of my family, I began to get anxious. Worrying about my family was something I always did well!

"Something has happened," I thought.

By then the sidewalks were empty of spectators and traffic was again rolling on the streets. The parade was definitely and officially over and my family hadn't been in it!

As I stood there searching the distant parade route and visualizing one of my kids splattered on the hard street and stepped on by a horse, I saw movement 'way down at the end of the street. As they approached slowly, I made out a black and white pony, a palomino mare, and a bay gelding. I breathed a sigh of relief, nothing had happened. Or as Joe described it later, *one* thing had occurred, over, and over, and over again.

Jan was wearing an extra-wide brimmed hat that had been given to her by a friend and which she had insisted on wearing in the parade. It was too big for her little head but Daddy put some "fit" (folded strips of newspaper under the sweatband) into it. It helped some but it was still a little loose and the wind kept catching the big brim and blowing the hat to the ground.

Each time it happened Joe would have to get off his horse, retrieve the hat, return it to Jan, remount, and continue. He couldn't carry the hat because he had his hands full with his reins and Steve in front of him. I didn't ask why he didn't just leave it lying on the street but then supposed that if Jan would have let him, that's possibly what he would have done.

Doggedly they continued on, getting further and further behind the parade until finally they were all alone.

Nevertheless, they had come to ride in the parade, and ride they did. That day the Barthles had their own private parade along the entire parade route. The kids, at least Jan and Steve, were happy they got to "ride in the parade." Randy, being older, wasn't as pleased at how things went.

As time passed and the kids became old enough to ride by themselves, with 4-H or FFA mounted groups, or eventually, not to want to ride at all, Joe and I helped decorate and ride on the floats of the Cattlemen and CattleWomen. The fun we had and the things that went wrong could have filled a book—a comic book at that!

For a few years we didn't take part in the parade at all. I guess it was because we were too busy or, more likely, we were just burned out on parades.

When our grandchildren reached the age where they wanted to participate, Joe had the brainstorm of renting an authentic stagecoach, complete with a driver and his sidekick, pulled by mules. He thought it would be fun for the kids, everybody could ride, and it would eliminate hauling horses to town.

Having firmly declined an offer to ride in the coach,

I felt reasonably safe in going to the lineup with a supply of candy for the kids to toss to other children along the parade route. Nevertheless, knowing my cowboy well, I had on a leather fringed jacket and jeans "just in case" he gently insisted.

But it was Larry who stated adamantly, "I think Papa Joe and Meemaw should be the one to ride with the kids. After all, they're the ones who started this bunch." So we rode in the parade.

The red stagecoach with the driver and his sidekick was identified on both sides as an entry of Barthle Brothers Ranch. It also had a sign on the back urging, "Raise your family, as we are, with the goodness of beef." We always take every opportunity we have to promote our product!

Clint, who was ten, and Nick, eight, were perched on the top of the coach on a bale of hay with their unloaded BB guns to "ride shotgun." Inside with Joe and me were six little ones, ranging in age from two to seven, all dressed in their jeans, boots, and hats. All, that is, except the two little girls who were beautiful in their colorful can-can saloon dancer outfits.

With a kid or two dangling from each window and two on top we must have resembled nothing more than the old woman who lived in a shoe and her husband who is never mentioned in the nursery rhyme. I often wondered where he lived but, thank goodness, no kid ever asked me that question.

Eight kids can toss a lot of candy and we learned that day to either get twice as much or none at all. There was no slowing them down once they got started.

"Save some for later in the parade," we kept telling them.

But they threw the last of it out about the half-way mark of the parade. As they all dismounted from the coach after the parade, we discovered that each of them had somehow managed to squirrel a few pieces away inside a hat or pocket for later enjoyment.

It was fun to ride along, recognizing and greeting friends. We all enjoyed it but I was relieved when the end came and neither of our two protectors on the roof had hurtled past the windows to decorate the street! From the banging and framming up there it had sounded as if they were either dancing or wrestling!

We were pleasantly surprised when the judges awarded us first place in the "Best Western Rig" category and we treasure the trophy as a memory of a good day spent with the grandchildren.

TRAGEDY

1985 began as a great year. Cassandra was born in April and Christopher arrived in June: Cassie and Chris. Mark and Tammy were married in May and our youngest, nineteen-year-old Beth, was engaged. She and her fiancee, Dennis, had set their wedding date for the following May and wedding plans were under way.

Then tragedy struck. Beth had flown to Louisville, Kentucky, with the owner of our neighboring ranch to see her fiancee, who was on the cattle show circuit. It was her first plane trip of any kind.

On the way back that night the plane crashed. Also on board were the ranch foreman, his wife, and a Mississippi cattleman.

It didn't seem real when we were wakened in the early morning hours with the news that the plane had crashed into a mountainside in North Carolina. Beth was gone.

Nature has a way of insulating us from grief that is too terrible to bear. The first days and weeks, even months, were spent in a state of numbed shock, not only by Joe and me, but the entire family. Beth had, after all, been the well loved baby of the family.

As for me, I moved, talked, and did the things I had to do, I suppose, but only by instinct or at the direction of others.

After the funeral, when the rest of the family and our friends had to return to their homes to try to pick up their lives again, all I wanted to do was to be alone with my grief. But, because I knew that in order to survive I had to keep myself busy, I tried to fill each hour of the day with as much activity as was possible.

I had fulfilled my lifetime ambition of becoming a journalist and was doing a commentary column and feature articles for *The Independent Farmer and Rancher*, a weekly agricultural paper. I had also been elected to serve on the Executive Committee of the American National CattleWomen. I guess God must have planned it because that work and my part-time employment as parish secretary at St. Anthony's Church is what kept me going for the next year or so.

Looking back, I can recognize that grieving had several distinct stages during that first year: shock, tentative belief, bitterness, denial, and finally, acceptance.

In the days and weeks after Beth's death, friends who had lost their own child came to us to offer comfort. Some said, "It will never get better."

Others told us, "It will always hurt, but eventually the pain will deaden to a dull ache."

Our pastor counseled, "It will take at least a year for you to even start to get over it."

They were right. After a year it still hurt but the truly devastating times didn't come as often. Even yet, when the realization hits that Beth is really gone, the pain is just as great.

The shock of loss is renewed at unexpected times and places by unexpected things: A hymn in Church. A young girl's hands with long slender fingers. Clothes in a store that would be just right for her. Her favorite foods in the grocery store or when I am cooking. A girl saying in a tone of exasperation and embarrassment, "Mo-o-om," almost making three syllables out of the word. A girl in an FFA jacket. Her favorite TV programs and music. Denny, her dog. A little gray Chevette. Her friends, bridal showers, weddings, and beauty pageants. Anything and everything.

A mother and father can cling together as they share the loss of their child, but each can hurt only for their own self, not for the other.

Each child has an equal and unique place in a parent's heart and love. Sons and daughters can give comfort to their parents but they cannot fill the void left by the loss of one of them. That particular spot will always remain empty except for memories. Nor can parents replace a beloved sister in their children's lives and hearts, no more than they can replace each other.

Friends can share and help with the load of sorrow, but

they cannot take it upon their own shoulders to bear. The love and sharing of family and friends helps, but in the final analysis each person has to face the reality of their loss and learn to deal with it in his or her own way, alone.

During the first year there were many times when I felt as if I were getting to my feet only to be knocked down again emotionally. All of the "firsts" without Beth had to be faced: holidays, birthdays, her wedding date. The loss of two other young people we knew, the loss of a couple who were our friends in a plane crash, and the explosion of the Space Shuttle were some of the events that were especially traumatic for me that year.

Sometimes I felt like a lone oak tree in the middle of an empty field with the winds of a storm battering me. And I would think, "Dear, God, I can't survive one more blow." But I did.

A friend asked how I was.

I smiled and said, "Fine."

She replied, "Someday you will smile and say that, and mean it."

And with the grace of God and the help of family and friends, that time came.

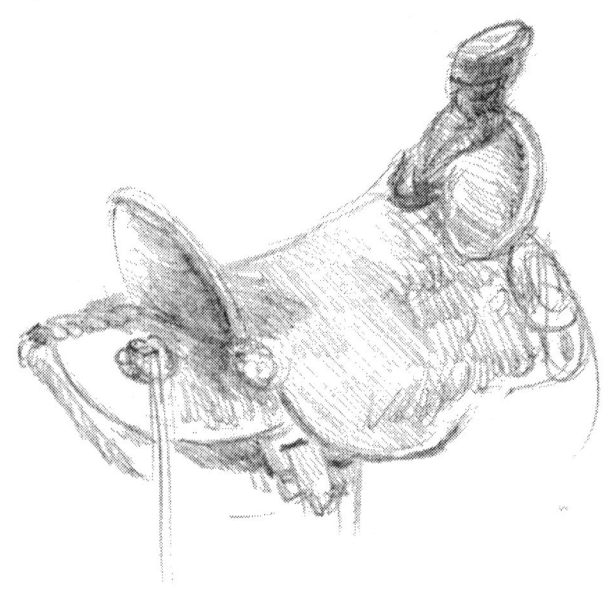

A WILD CHASE

For some reason our horses seem to know when I'm at home by myself. It's obvious that they do because that's when they manage to find a way out of their pasture or the barn, and wander off down the road.

Cows do, too, of course, but they're more placid and it's easier to get them to go back where they should be. Usually they will just go through or over a fence and into a pasture, not necessarily the one they just came from. Cows don't seem to care if they're in a different field and I sure don't either. It's all the same to me which grass they graze on for a few hours, as long as they're off the hard road so they don't get hit or cause an accident.

Horses are different. As they are a more spirited animal, they enjoy running up and down the road, dashing past all of the open gates and lanes into which they could, or should, turn. Either they don't see the inviting open gaps in the fence line, or they don't think that what they are looking for lies in that direction.

One particular day when I was home alone someone had left the milk cow's stall door open and seven of our best Quarter Horses found their way through that door from their pasture. I didn't know they were loose until I heard the thunder of their hooves and their shrill whinnying as they galloped past the house and down the lane to freedom.

As I raced to the car I breathed a prayer that I would be able to get past them and "cut 'em off at the pass," that being the hard road.

Down at the end of the lane is the county graded road. The hard road, which has quite a few speeding cars whizzing by, is one-half mile to the east. I thought I was in luck that day when after pausing to investigate matters, all seven of the horses turned west. In that direction, about one-half mile away, there is a metal cattleguard between us and Stage Coach Ranch.

I was sure that when the horses reached the cattle guard, they would stop and I could herd them back home. Was I ever mistaken! I didn't know it then, but my difficulties were just beginning!

As they journeyed down the road, with fences on each side, it was almost as if those aggravating horses were playing a teasing game with me. They would trot a little bit, then stop to nibble at the grass. Suddenly, one of them would snort and take off at a run with the others hightailing after him.

When I finally caught up with the runaways, they were resting at the cattle guard and restoring their energy by picking at the fresh green grass on either side of the road. Easing past, I turned the car around to start them back, hoping that when they reached our lane they would be cooperative enough to turn down it.

Obediently, but slowly, they moved off in the right direction. I breathed a sigh of relief that turned out to be premature. Two of them suddenly jumped and raced back past the car towards the cattle guard.

Hastily scrambling out of the car, I tried to turn them back, but they were too fast for me. All I could do at that point was to stand there with my heart in my throat, almost forgetting to breathe. Two very valuable roping horses were picking their way across the cattle guard! They weren't jumping it, which wouldn't have been as bad if they took a long enough jump, those two were walking it!

I was afraid that if I moved at all one or both might miss a step and have their leg slip through the bars and break.

Somehow they made it safely across without mishap and began grazing quietly on our neighbor's lush grass, completely unaware of my racing pulse, rapid heart beat, and elevated blood pressure.

"O.K." I thought. "Happy grazing."

Two were off the road and I decided they could stay there 'til the men came home. I backed my car onto the cattle guard to keep the others from trying the same trick, and I set off afoot to try to finish the job of herding them back home.

I had left home so quickly that I hadn't taken time to put

shoes on so I was still wearing flimsy house slippers, not exactly the footwear in which to trail horses. The only solution was to take them off, so I started off barefoot down the road after the horses with whom I was rapidly losing patience.

Right then a surprising thing happened! A young man who was working on another ranch in the area came by and stopped, after I had waved him down. I described what had happened and told him that the keys were in my car if he wanted to move it to get across the cattle guard. The surprising thing was that that's just what he did, with no offer to help me with the horses.

It's unusual for a ranch person not to offer assistance to someone who was so obviously in need of help. That's just not in the nature of the species!

The other five horses meandered slowly back down the road and I didn't attempt to hurry them because I positively didn't want them to spook again. When they reached the open gate leading to Randy's home they opted to turn into it.

Randy and Patty had only recently moved into their new home and hadn't done any landscaping yet, so I knew there were no plants for the horses to eat or trample.

Thankfully, I shut them in, trudged back to my car, and went home, leaving them to mow Randy's grass.

Three hours later when the boys came home they were surprised to see our horses scattered all around. But, without asking any questions, they gathered them up and put them back where they belonged. It was so easy for them; they were cowboys, born and bred.

Chasing kids was more in my line of experience. I might not have always had an easy time getting the youngsters to go where I wanted them to be or do what I wanted them to do, but they were a lot easier to handle! At least they understood English and knew what a spanking was!

SOMETHING GOT A HOLD ON ME

One of the advantages of living in the country is the abundance of interesting places to walk. When I'm in town and see the unfortunate city people doing their daily mile or so on cement sidewalks or race tracks I really do feel sympathy for them.

Here on the ranch I can choose between walking down the dirt road, circling the pond, or rambling through the woods. Even if for some reason or other I need to stay close to the house while I am walking my two miles, there's almost always something interesting to see. On just one walk I saw a coon, an armadillo, and assorted birds, in addition to the cattle and horses.

Walking out of the woods one day onto a little field, I surprised three deer that were placidly grazing on the luscious green rye. Startled, their heads came up at the same instant they moved into motion. It was a tossup as to who was the most excited, them or me. My reaction was to stand still as they left at a run! The last glimpse I had of them was of their white tails as they sailed over a fence and disappeared into the woods.

Two fox, apparently playing near their den, weren't aware of me until I was fairly close. After they sighted me quietly enjoying the beauty of their red coats glinting in the sunshine, they raced away and ran for about one-eighth of a mile before stopping in the shade of a tree and eyeing me warily. I assumed they were trying to draw me away from their young so I continued on my way without further investigation, letting them return to their undisturbed den.

Coons, who don't see too well, don't appear to spot me until I'm almost on top of them. When they finally do see me, they usually scamper to the nearest tree and hide.

'Possums and armadillos, though, seem to be in their own world. I guess they are marching to their own drumbeat. Nothing seems to excite them too much, and they just amble along their way, tending to their own business and leaving me to tend to mine.

Luckily I haven't seen a snake, but not because I haven't looked for them. I keep a wary eye out, glancing ahead and to the sides as I go. It's not that I dislike snakes; I don't have any feeling about them one way or the other as long as I see one in time to avoid stepping on it.

In the spring it's pleasant to go by the horse pasture to see if there are new foals and to check on how the older ones are coming along. Newborn foals are so ugly and awkward that they are cute, at least to me. Their legs are skinny and spread addled as they try to stand, and it's amazing how quickly they get their feet squarely under them and start frolicking around.

Fall brings new calves and I think they are beautiful from birth! It's really heartwarming to see a mama cow placidly washing her newborn baby. It's a tribute to her mothering instinct, that even when she leaves it lying up somewhere while she grazes, she always knows exactly where it is and comes running if she senses danger to it.

As I walk down the dirt road I look for tracks in the sand: a long squiggly line left by a snake; the delicate markings of a quail; occasionally a deer, coon, or 'possum track; and even traces of little bugs. I don't always know which is which, but I enjoy looking for them and guessing what they might be.

The roadsides and woods are full of wild flowers. To have the opportunity to examine and enjoy them up close is another bonus of walking in the country. Sometimes I return home with an armload of Black-eyed Susans and some nameless, to me, purple flowers with which I fill vases to brighten up the house. Golden rod is a "no-no" since I'm allergic to it but I can enjoy it from the safety of distance.

One night I received more excitement than I expected, or

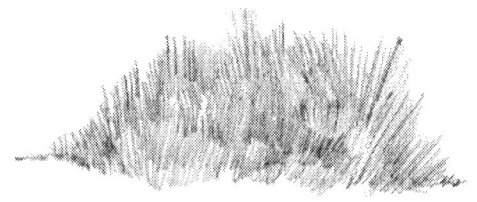

wanted. I had walked further than I had intended and it was already dark as I neared home. All of a sudden something jumped out from the side of the road and grabbed my ankle!

I was so scared that I must have jumped three feet and screeched like a banshee! Then I heard a gentle meow and a playful rubbing on my leg and realized that it was only Al come to greet and play with me. That was one walk I returned from with my heart beating fast and my circulatory system working overtime.

When my doctor ordered me to start taking long brisk walks daily I thought, "Oh no! Another chore to add to my already busy days!"

Now I've come to enjoy and look forward to my walks as a time of peace and relaxation. They are a welcome interlude in the sometimes hectic pace of life. Sometimes it's hard to find the time for walks, but when I do I come home refreshed both physically and mentally after my brief sojourn with nature.

Hard Work For A Good Life

Summer is the time for hard, dirty work on a ranch. Well, really, there isn't any time when it's not busy on a Florida ranch.

Maybe it just seems like everybody is working harder in the summer time because they get so dirty and sweaty then. In Florida the heat and humidity saps the energy, leaving both humans and animals tired and drained by the end of the day.

Iced tea, cold drinks, and water are consumed by the gallons each day during the hot months. It seems superfluous to use the adjective "iced" because most Florida Crackers assume that "iced" is part of "tea." "Cold drink" or "coke" (never "pop" or "soda") is used to describe just about any kind of carbonated soft drink.

At any rate, almost every time someone comes by the house, they make a quick stop to grab a glass of cold refreshment. If they're in a hurry, they take along a drink on the way to another job that needed to be done yesterday!

I keep a supply of one quart glasses and periodically have to send out a plea to "please look in all of the trucks, in the machine shop, and in the barns for my glasses and bring them back so I can wash them and have them ready for use again." Throwaway plastic cups weren't the answer because, as I was told, "They're too small."

Summer is the primary time when the cows are penned and worked. When it's time to do all of this, everyone who's big enough to ride a horse alone, and at least follow along, helps.

If they're not old enough, nor experienced enough, to go into the oak thickets and palmetto patches to bring out cattle, they "plug a hole" in the line to keep the cattle from cutting back.

The kids always think it's a "grown up" thing to graduate from "bringing up the rear" to being a vital part of the roundup crew and get right in the middle of the action.

Boys or girls, they all help. As the grandkids get older they are beginning to take part in the roundups, too.

My contribution is lunch. Before the children were old enough to pitch in, we hired day help and I cooked and carried lunch to the entire crew at the pens five miles down in the pasture. As our family grew and started helping themselves, the girls and I began packing lunches for them to take along.

The girls could saddle their own horses, but in an effort to divide the chores, the boys saddled up and made sure all of the needed equipment and supplies were loaded while the girls helped me.

Another part of my job, and one which I have always taken quite seriously, is worrying. *Somebody* has to worry about whether everybody is going to get home uninjured, and who can do the job better than good ole Mom?

After the riders make a sweep through a large pasture to bring out the cattle, they eat lunch in the shade at the cowpens. In the afternoon they either "work" the cows they have penned or make another drive and work them all the next day.

Because of my other duties, like having babies and looking after toddlers, I've never been able to get to the cowpens often but I've heard a lot about it and understand the kids have a wonderful time.

In between "helping," they ride calves, rope each other and the dogs, dunk one another in the water trough, and do all the other "fun" things that ranch kids love to do.

One of them informed me once in what I considered to be a rather smug manner, "Mom, it's a good thing you're not there or we'd never have any fun. You'd have us all sitting in the truck all day so we wouldn't get hurt."

They did have their share of bumps, kicks, scrapes, and falls which were sometime, but not often, bad enough for a trip to the doctor or emergency room. Thankfully, none have been injured seriously or permanently.

Our girls loved working cattle as much as the boys did and they were always delighted to escape household chores because, "Daddy needs me." Ranch girls learn at an early age that housework can be done any time but cow work can't.

Winter is the time of the year when one would think that the workload would ease off. The hay is in, the last calves are weaned, pastures are mowed, and there's no major cow work to be done.

The pace probably is a little less hectic than in the summer. With days being shorter it must be or there wouldn't be time to get all the work finished.

Then, again, with less hours of sunlight, sometimes the work doesn't get finished. The absolutely necessary things are done, even when it means staying at it until well after dark, but other jobs that aren't on the top of the priority list may be put off until there's time to do them. One thing is sure, there's never a time when a rancher can get up in the morning and say, "I don't have anything to do today." There's always work to be done.

Even in Florida, especially after a heavy frost or freeze, there is a shortage of grass in the winter. One of the things that has to be done every day is the "feeding up." Truck loads of hay and molasses or mineral blocks are taken to the cattle in the pastures. The bulls, heifers, and registered cattle get feed with their hay as well as mineral supplement every day.

There are also some animals in the feedlot during the winter, usually late calves that weren't big, or "bloomy" enough to sell with the big bunch in the fall. They, too, have to be fed, hayed, and watered each day. While doing all of that, the animals are carefully checked to make sure none are sick.

If there's enough rain for the grass to grow there are winter rye fields, which means we turn the heifers into the field to graze each day and take them off before dark so they won't lie down and trample the grass.

There's also a rye field for the cows and their new calves which start dropping in late November. The cows have to be paired with their calves and moved to pastures where they have access to both a rye and a water supply.

The herd of registered Brahman cows must be checked each day to tattoo new calves and record them for registration.

There are always fences that need to be mended or rebuilt, and trucks and equipment that are constantly breaking down have to be repaired. Machinery repair usually involves at least one trip, sometimes more, to town for parts. Sometimes a specific part is hard to find, and they don't always fit after you get home with them!

Since my mechanical knowledge is in the zero range, I have learned from experience to insist that the mechanic on duty that day call the parts store and determine what they want. All I have to do then is pick it up. I don't have to make the decision of whether a one and five-eighths bolt will do if they don't have a one and one-half inch one in stock!

Pumps deep in the pasture must be visited quite often to make sure they are still pumping water for the cattle to drink, especially in times of drought when the ponds and lakes are dried up. Our area is often hit by tropical storms and pumps are a prime lightning target.

Foals that have been weaned have to be fed each day and gentled to allow a halter to be put on them. There are always horses in training for riding or roping or dogging and, one hopes, to sell to a rodeo contestant.

Now that we've added a shade house to grow indoor foliage, it sometimes involves everyone's pitching in for a day or so to "stick" cuttings in pots or "pull" plants for shipping. Sometimes, if an unexpected cold spell is moving in earlier than usual and the heaters and plastic covering for the shade house haven't been installed, it's a first priority to get that done so the plants don't freeze.

Every time plants are "pulled" for sale, they have to be replaced by new ones to grow. Cuttings are "stuck" in a pot of peat and placed in the propagation house where an automatic sprinkler system sprays them with a fine mist every few minutes until they have a good root system. Then they are moved to the shade house to grow until they are the desired size for sale.

To the uninitiated, ranching appears to be a romantic way of life: living in the beautiful country with nothing to do but sit back, watch your cattle grow, and haul them to market to sell.

Caring for animals is hard work but ranchers do it in order to give their livestock the very best care they can. If they didn't have a love for animals and for the way of life, they wouldn't be in the business!

It is not only in the animal's interest to be well fed, watered, and disease free, it assures the rancher that he will have the safest, most wholesome product to market to the consumer who will purchase it.

Ranch living is a good way of life, a good way to raise children, and most ranch families, including ours, wouldn't trade that way of life for any other.

I'M ALL RIGHT, IT'S JUST A SCRATCH

There's probably not a ranch wife and mother anywhere who doesn't consider it to be the normal thing when bruised, battered, and sometimes bloody cowboys and cowgirls come home to be cleaned up, diagnosed, and lavished with sympathy. Sometimes just a kiss where it hurts, a hug, and a bandaid is all that is needed to make everything better. At other times it takes more. . .a lot more.

At our house the final decision on the seriousness of the injury tended to rest with Daddy if he were home. He'd say something like, "He'll be all right, just had the wind knocked out of him." Or, "It's just a bump on the head, she'll be okay." Or, "It doesn't need stitches. We'll just pull the edges together with some tape. It'll heal just fine. "

His favorite advice to the injured was, "Just think how good it will feel when it quits hurting!" That didn't help the hurt right then but it usually brought a reluctant smile to the kids and gave them something to think about!

I was pretty good at cleaning and bandaging wounds or changing bandages and dispensing medications when needed. I was excellent at giving hugs, kisses, and bandaids but when it came to applying "butterfly" bandages, Joe was better. Somehow, I never could hold the edges together and apply the tape just right.

Occasionally in the case of bad cuts, concussions, or broken bones, we were off for another trip to the doctor's office or the hospital emergency room.

The incidence of agriculture-related accidents is high, right at the top of the chart. Because of the very nature of the work with livestock and equipment, some are unavoidable.

Many are caused by some degree of carelessness while using equipment, or are the end result of trying to "out think" animals. Cowboys who have worked with livestock for their entire lives are good at doing that: trying to out think animals. At least they reach a point where they think that they pretty well know how an animal will react and what it will do in a given circumstance.

That's good. It's a necessary characteristic of a real topnotch cowboy. It's those times when a horse or cow doesn't do what it's presumed to have been programmed to do that accidents happen. As I've pontificated many times, "People don't act predictable all the time, so how can we expect it of an animal?"

Over the years we've had our share of injuries, some at work and some at play. Some were serious and others not so bad. With a cowboy daddy and seven normal, energetic youngsters, it's to be expected that accidents will happen, and I definitely did come to expect them!

There was a memorable Sunday morning when our family went into church looking as though we were survivors from a war or disaster area. Joe was on crutches with a white sock adorning one foot. Larry's arm had a cast on it and he wore it in a sling, and Mark's hand was heavily bandaged.

Joe had been pushing a corner pull post out of the back of his pickup truck. The post was made from part of a discarded telephone pole and was large and heavy. All of a sudden it hit a snag in the bed of the truck, jerked out of his hands, and dropped onto his foot, crushing his big toe.

Larry had stuck his arm between two boards of the chute while urging a cow to "move on." She moved, all right, and slammed his arm against the board and broke it. He learned a lesson that day: put your arm over, not through a fence when working cattle.

Mark, a little fellow of nine, had lost part of a finger when for some reason known only to him, he reached into the feed mixer to pick out a piece of feed. We never did find out why he felt the need to get it out of the mixer rather than from the full bag of feed on the floor. He was lucky that he hadn't lost an arm!

I think that was the only time we had multiple injuries. Other accidents of varying degrees of seriousness happened fairly regularly, or maybe it just seemed that way since there were so many of us.

When Steve was five and Jan was seven they decided to have a race to reach the ground from the top of the gym set. Steve jumped to the ground and won the race. His prize was a broken arm and a trip to the hospital! He had already survived, unscathed, a plunge from the hayloft with a bundle of loose hay accompanying him to cushion his fall. We never did establish, at least not to my satisfaction, whether he jumped, fell, or was pushed. It seemed to be one of those things that was better left alone!

Jan's collarbone was broken when she fell out of bed and her shoulder ligaments were torn when Randy twisted her arm while they were playing. She also injured her back as a teenager when she bounced off the tailgate of a pickup; luckily it wasn't moving fast.

Kathy bruised her kidneys and Steve got a concussion when their horses, which they were riding bareback, ran away with them and they fell off. Steve was not only bareback, he didn't even have a halter or bridle on his horse! Not being there I don't know how that came about. Probably someone dared him to do it, so when Daddy wasn't looking he just jumped on his horse and raced off. And Fell Off! And spent the night in the hospital.

Randy broke his ankle playing football but his most embarrassing injury occurred when he sat on a nail which was sticking up in a board. While that might have been his most embarrassing injury, it didn't compare in seriousness with the nail he stepped on that was in another board. That time he ended up in the hospital some weeks later for surgery to remove a small bit of sock that had been carried deep into his foot by the nail and was embedded, causing infection and some bone damage.

Mark had a broken arm when his horse bucked him off during a sudden thunderstorm, and Joe's ankle was broken when he tried to turn a thoroughbred mare back by stepping out in front of her.

Good old faithful Blondie, our dog, who was so patient and good with the kids, unpredictably bit Randy for teasing him while he was eating. With blood streaming down Randy's face we had a scary few minutes until we ascertained that the bite was over his eye, not in it, and didn't require stitches.

Randy cracked a hip when he was bucked off by a young horse that he was in the process of breaking. By then he was grown and had acquired the cowboy mind set of "Don't go to the doctor as long as you can walk, don't need any stitches, and can talk!" Ten years later he developed arthritis which was caused by that injury and an assortment of other football and rodeo injuries. Eventually, he required a hip replacement.

Steve lost part of a toe when a weight fell off the rack in the gym where he was working out.

When Beth ate some berries from a lariope plant and we were concerned that they might be poisonous, we had the Extension Agent check it out for us and pronounce the little purple berries harmless. Beth was the one who liked to eat things: she grabbed a handful of dishwasher detergent out of the machine while I was filling it and burned her mouth and throat severely. When I called the local doctor, he advised that I take her immediately to a hospital in Tampa. Since there wasn't anyone at home to go with me, she and I took the forty mile trip alone. As I drove well beyond the speed limit, her throat became so swollen that whenever she tried to swallow she just kind of gurgled. I thought she was going to choke or asphyxiate before we could get to the hospital! As it turned out, she didn't receive any treatment but wasn't able to eat or drink anything for several days. She would cry in hunger and pain and then cry more when she tried to eat even the most bland or cooling foods we offered. Then the first food she ate, which she asked for, was POPCORN!

Beth even tried to take a bath in Saniflush one day! I was always careful to keep those kinds of things locked away but children are so quick to get them if they are left out for just a minute. She got the Saniflush when I put it down on the dining room table between cleaning bathrooms. She poured the pretty blue "bubble bath" into her bath water and climbed in. Luckily I was pretty close and pulled her out at once.

These weren't all of our kid's accidents by any means, just a few! Even Mom had one! While I was painting the eaves of the carport one day, I missed the bottom rung of the ladder, caught my foot in it, did a flip, and landed hard on my posterior. Anyone driving up right then would have had to laugh! There I sat, paint brush still in my hand, with paint splattered all over me, crying! It hurt! Bad!

The full effects on my body hadn't set in yet so after a while I got up, crawled back up on the ladder, and finished the job. It was a good thing I did because for the next week or so I could hardly walk, stand, bend, sit, or even move!

And I didn't go to the doctor either!

I have found that the hardest part of caring for a sick or injured cowboy is keeping him still. It's almost impossible to get one to go to the doctor. If they finally see one, the average cowboy is convinced that he knows better than the doctor what he can do. And then usually does it!

One afternoon Joe got bucked off a young horse he was training and got knocked literally silly. He didn't have any idea what had happened, nor how he and his horse got back to the barn, but he knew where he had lost his hat!

And he giggled. . .and giggled, all during supper until Grandma finally asked me, "Is he drinking?"

Refusing to go to the doctor, he just kept repeating, over and over, "I'm all right." I sure couldn't pick him up and carry him, so I got in touch with one of the two doctors I felt that I knew well enough to call. . .our pediatrician. The other one was my gynecologist but, given the patient, I opted for the kid's doctor.

Dr. Baggs said, "He probably should go in for X-rays and observation, but if he won't go, watch his eyes, and wake him every few hours tonight to make sure he *will* wake up and is all right."

I set the alarm and woke him up with no trouble. I reset the alarm and went back to sleep. The second time it went off, he shook me awake.

"I'm all right"' he assured me.

The day he didn't open a gate was different.

Heifers were being moved from one large pasture to another and Joe was supposed to ride ahead to hold them in and open the gate for the crew to push them on in. When the rest of the crew got there the heifers were scattered all over, the gate was shut, and there was no Daddy in sight. That definitely was not typical, so they began a search.

Several hours after the accident had probably occurred, Randy found his horse standing with head hanging low. He was covered with dried sweat and sand. Nearby on the ground was Joe's hat. There was still no Daddy to be seen. But after much calling, they finally located him sitting under a tree as if he didn't have a thing in the world to do!

"What are you doing, Daddy?" Randy asked.

"I guess I just took a nap," he replied.

He was dirty, scratched, and bruised and his shirt was torn. He had no idea what had happened to him but was most emphatic and adamant on one point: "I'm all right."

After they got him in the truck and brought him home, I cleaned him up a little and told him, "We're going to go to the hospital."

"I don't need to go. I'm all right. It's just some scratches," he insisted.

"We're going. That's that and I don't intend to argue about it," I stated flatly.

As noted, Daddy usually made the final decisions on seeking medical treatment, but this time I did. However, I did find it amusing to hear one of the little kids say to another, "Did you hear how Mama talked to Daddy?"

I guess that pretty well tells the story of who was king of

the Barthle castle. Still, where there is a king, there's usually a queen!

After X-rays and examination he should have been admitted for observation. However, the young doctor in the emergency room apparently wasn't familiar with a cowboy's medical philosophy. He took Joe at his word when he reiterated, "I'm all right. It just hurts a little bit," and let him come home.

It took about three weeks for that beat up cowboy to get over that wreck. He was sore all over and had to get out of bed one muscle at a time! Of course, he should have stayed in bed at least for a few days but that would have been asking too much of a hard-headed cowboy!

He slept a lot, anywhere at any time, but was real easy to wake up and talked sensibly.

The next day, Joe insisted that he was going out in the pasture in his pickup to check on those heifers. I asked Jan to go along to drive, open and shut gates, and to be sure he came home!

He never did remember what happened but we guessed from the evidence that while his horse was running as they tried to turn the heifers, it stepped in a gopher hole, fell and rolled on Joe. We were lucky.

Cowboys hate to get hurt and, what's more, they don't like to admit that they are injured, at least not until after they're all healed. What they do enjoy is talking about their accidents later with other cowboys. When two or more of them get together, the wrecks they have had is the third most popular topic of conversation with them—right after the weather and price of cattle and just before their horses, dogs, wives, and family!

A Bizarre Accident

Occasionally an accident on a ranch surpasses the unusual and borders on the bizarre. Thus it was when Chick Black took a notion to revert to pre-historic times and act like he was a dinosaur.

For a long while Chick had been the only stallion at the barn and was indisputably the king among his harem of mares and fillies. But a few months previously all of that had changed when Joe purchased a two-year old stallion and brought him home to the barn.

The blue roan was a son of our Wrangler from a mare that he had serviced while we still owned him. While Joe had no intention to use him as a sire, he thought Thunder would be a good mount to use for riding and working cattle.

Chick, of course, couldn't know that Thunder was not there to compete in his amorous duties and saw him only as a threat to his own status as king. He took an instant dislike to Thunder and the feeling was definitely mutual!

Chick was much the bigger of the two horses, standing at fifteen hands, three inches, and weighing 1200 pounds. Thunder, though he was only fourteen hands, two inches, and tipped the scales at 1000 pounds, didn't usually back off from Chick.

The new horse was scheduled to be neutered but, with one thing and another, several months passed before it was done. As time passed, Chick's dislike for Thunder grew into a vicious and active hate.

Even after Thunder had been gelded and was no longer a potential challenge to Chick as a stallion, the two continued to be antagonists. Chick would show his outrage at the intruder's presence with loud squeals and snorts and by charging in to attack Thunder at every opportunity.

One afternoon, as the sun was just reaching the tops of the trees in the West, Joe and Tommy Diffenwierth, a young man who was helping us at the time, were riding their horses back to the barn through the horse pasture. They had been working cattle and were heading home, tired and dirty.

Chick, who had been grazing in the pasture, also sensed that it was nearing the end of the day. Having slowly worked his way back to the barn, stopping occasionally to pick another mouthful of grass, he was waiting outside the barn to be placed in his stall and fed. Seeing Chick grazing near the barn, Joe told Tommy, "Chick will be wanting to fight Thunder. If you'll swing your rope around overhead it will keep him away."

As soon as Chick spied Joe and Tommy walking their horses side-by-side across the field, he came running. Wanting to give Tommy room to swing his rope around himself and Thunder, Joe dropped behind him.

Seeing Chick circle to the left, and thinking that he had scared him away, Tommy stopped swinging his rope. That turned out to be a big mistake because by then Chick was almost directly behind him. Whirling quickly, Chick charged in, trying to bite Thunder.

Of course Thunder couldn't be expected to just stand still while he was being attacked! His instinctive and sudden movement spoiled Chick's aim and whatever his target might have been, neck or rump, he missed. Instead, his wide-opened jaws clamped down on Tommy's thigh!

Tommy was not a tall man but he wasn't exactly small either. He stood about five feet, six inches tall, weighed 160 pounds, and was well built and stocky.

As noted, Chick was a big horse. With no effort at all, and without even pausing, he picked Tommy up from the saddle and trotted away with him. There was Tommy, dangling from Chick's mouth, with his head hanging down and his arms swinging! Joe and Tommy later described the sight as a living example of scenes from a science fiction movie depicting a dinosaur moving along, carrying his victim in his mouth!

Chick trotted along for about twenty feet before finally

lowering his head and gently placing Tommy on the ground. He didn't drop him, he just put him down nice and easy, almost as if he were apologizing to Tommy for having bothered him!

"He wasn't trying to hurt Tommy," Joe said. "He just wanted to get at Thunder and Tommy got in the way."

After he had deposited Tommy on the ground, safely out of the way, Chick whirled back with a loud squeal to continue his attack on Thunder.

In the meantime Joe had ridden up and caught Thunder's reins. He kept the two horses circling because as long as he and his horse remained between Chick and Thunder things were comparatively quiet. Thunder wasn't trying to fight anymore and appeared to want nothing more than to go to the barn!

Chick wasn't making any attempt to bite the horse Joe was riding but he kept circling, too, trying to find an opportunity to charge in again and attack Thunder once more.

Tommy, who must have been in terrible pain, managed to hobble into the barn and return with a cow whip. Popping it loudly over his head, he succeeded in scaring Chick away so that Joe could lead Thunder safely into the barn.

Tommy was wearing a brand new pair of jeans which Chick's teeth ripped apart but, although his entire thigh was very badly bruised, the skin was not torn. A trip to the doctor and a week off from work made him right as rain. It could definitely have been worse!

That episode had a sequel, as so many things do.

On another day, when Thunder had been a gelding for about eight months, Chick was again turned out into the pasture and Joe was riding Thunder, but in the other direction from the barn. Returning from the opposite end of the barn, he unsaddled Thunder and prepared to turn him into the pasture.

Joe led Thunder out through the wide barn door and to the gate of the lot behind the barn. Since the two enemies couldn't be loose in the pasture together he was going to let Chick come in first, intending to remove the halter from Thunder and turn him loose after Chick was safely inside.

Opening the long board gate that led into the lot from the pasture, and leaving the barn door open, Joe stood behind the gate with Thunder, waiting for chick to come in.

"I thought that with the gate between us he wouldn't try anything," Joe explained later.

Which, to a point, was right. Chick didn't pay any attention to Joe and Thunder and obediently trotted through the lot and started into the barn. Just then, before Joe had time to turn him loose, Thunder decided to do a little attacking of his own. He lunged at Chick.

Chick quite naturally couldn't resist the chance for a fight. He immediately whirled around to answer the challenge.

Quickly closing the gate, Joe was backed into the corner of the wooden pen, still holding Thunder, who stood between him and Chick.

As Chick lunged at him, Thunder dropped to his knees and Chick's mouth passed where Thunder had been standing a second before. Having missed his target, Chick's mouth, in a reflex action, closed and his teeth sank into Joe's arm.

Luckily, Chick didn't have his mouth wide open. If it had been, Joe's whole arm would have been in it and could have been badly mangled. As it was, Joe got a bad bite and lost a chunk out of his arm, which took a good bit of time to completely heal. He still bears the scars from that day, along with a lot more that have been acquired over the years.

Still holding Thunder's reins, Joe started hitting at Chick with them and ran him into the barn to his stall.

After turning Thunder out into the pasture, Joe fed his horses and came to the house for supper. To him, it was just another ordinary incident in a cowboy's life!

Some time later, we decided to get rid of Thunder and sold him to a friend who needed a gentle horse for his daughter to ride. And Thunder was gentle. So was Chick. It was just that, as is the case with some people, they just brought out the worst in each other!

WHAT'S IN A NAME?

I've always been partial to kittens, puppies, and calves, but my favorite newborn animals are foals. Each year it's a surprise all over again to see how fast a foal will grow and get muscled out. One day they're struggling as they try to stand and get their long wobbly legs square under them to search for their first meal. By the next week they're running all over the pasture, and soon after that they're trying out their new nipper teeth as they pick at the grass in their pasture.

For a few hours each day in the spring the mares and foals are turned into a rye field to benefit from the fresh new grass. I never tire of watching that scene: red, sorrel, black, and palomino mares and foals grazing on a bright carpet of green. The dark green trees at the edge of the pasture form a perfect frame for the little lake that is nestling in the background with its blue waters sparkling in the sunshine. That is nature at its best!

Many times I've tried to get near enough on foot or in the car to take pictures of the foals, but the mares always see me coming. Their heads come up as they look at me, whinny, and maneuver themselves between their babies and what they obviously consider to be a danger.

After all the mares have foaled we have the somewhat difficult chore of naming and registering them. It doesn't seem that it should be much of a job but sometimes it can be a gigantic one!

We often think of some really good names until the time comes to fill out the registration forms. Then our minds are a complete blank. That's when we get out the pedigrees of the sires and dams.

During our years of raising Quarter Horses we've had five stallions. Trying to incorporate five lines of breeding into the names of new foals can be quite frustrating at times.

First we had Wrangler who was by Roan Hancock. Wrangler was a sorrel with good conformation and a beautiful head. Although he was a little on the small side he threw good-sized foals and all of them inherited his speed and unbelievable stopping ability, a valued asset in a rope horse. Even generations later his descendants still have a natural stop.

In the early years of our marriage, before we had any neighbors or a telephone, Wrangler was my watch dog, or "watch horse." If a strange vehicle came down the lane, Wrangler would stick his head over the fence in his lot and whinny shrilly. He didn't pay any attention when one of our trucks or tractors came but seemed to want to let us know when a stranger was arriving.

One of our mares, Mui Bonita L, crossed well with him. Sometime later we bred a mare to Geech Partin's Misty Joe in Kissimmee so we got some of his bloodlines in there, too.

Many of the foals were named Wrangler's Misty, Wrangler's Bonita, Bonita's Wrangler, Misty's Wrangler, and so on. It could be confusing but those were just their official names. Each was known by its own recognizable name on the ranch.

Bonita lived to be twenty-two years old, giving us a foal almost every year. She was a long-coupled horse and as she aged and continued to foal each year she became more and more swaybacked.

Finally, at the age of twenty-two, after she threw her last foal, her back muscles simply gave out. She wasn't able to get up, and we put her painlessly to sleep.

Champ, the first good horse Joe had, was a particular favorite of his. After he was too old to be ridden anymore he was turned out in the pasture to live out the balance of his life in ease.

Chick Black, a bay, was a yearling when we bought him several years before Wrangler was sold. I watched in disappointment as Joe unloaded the gangly, long-legged colt, with what seemed to be a head like a mule's, from the trailer.

Not wanting to hurt Joe's feelings, I didn't say anything but, privately, I thought, "that has to be one of the ugliest horses around!" Which just proved that Joe knows his horseflesh and could visualize how Chick would develop. He turned out to be a big horse and well-proportioned. Crossed on Wrangler's daughters, he gave us some real good foals.

One day when Chick was about fifteen years old Joe had him on the trailer and was hauling him to the pasture to service the mares. A loud banging in the trailer didn't make much of an impression on Joe because he thought Chick was just getting excited and kicking. He was really surprised when he got to the mares' pasture and found Chick down. He died shortly of an apparent heart attack.

Then we bought Lucky Dude Bar. Although each have contributed good qualities to the herd, this one was the best. Wrangler's conformation, stop, and beautiful head, Chick's size, and Dude's outstanding conformation have really combined well.

Tiger, another sorrel, was next. He only lasted as a stallion for a couple of breeding seasons even though he was a good horse. He suffered from shyness with the girls so he was gelded, used for riding, and eventually sold.

Our latest acquisition is Sugar. He's still young and hasn't been used much as a sire yet but the foals we have from him show promise.

It's amazing how little a semi-town girl knows about horses and cattle when she first moves to the ranch. The language used in the business is an interesting study in itself.

Cattle are the easiest to learn about, I think. Joe would say, "Number 31 calved today. She had a bull calf," or a heifer, and I could easily understand that he meant one of the registered Brahman cows had a male or female calf. That's easier for a novice to catch on to than the terminology used for foals.

At first I thought that they were all colts. After a bit I learned that if Joe said a mare had a foal, it meant he hadn't gotten close enough to see the sex. If he did get near he would say, "Bonita had a colt or filly today."

It's simple, once you learn the language!

LONG NIGHT

After shutting Wrangler, a son of the original Wrangler, in his stall for feeding on a Friday evening, Joe went back to the barn after supper to turn him into the pasture to graze during the night.

He found Wrangler lying down and could see that he had been rolling, a classic symptom of colic in horses. Rolling completely over in an effort to ease the pain doesn't seem to do the damage to a horse that rolling back and forth on their back with a rocking motion does. That can often result in a twisted intestine, prevent the animal from having a bowel movement, or cause more severe problems.

Colic is pain in the abdominal area that can be the result of any number of things: eating indigestible or spoiled food can cause it, as can drinking too soon after eating, or when overheated or tired. Overeating, a sudden change in the diet, eating too fast, working too soon after a full feed, or standing idle with a full stomach are also possibilities for causing colic.

Sometimes a habit of a particular horse is the culprit. A horse will occasionally like to "crib" or chew on wood—either a fence post or its feedbox.

"Windsucking" or drawing in a belly full of air, or faulty or incomplete chewing of food because of diseased or mal-formed teeth can also be reasons for the painful condition. We surmised that Wrangler's colic had been caused by a recent change in the kind of oats he was being fed.

Colic is a worrisome experience for the horse's owners because the ailment is so often fatal. In fact, it is probably the leading cause of death in horses.

Luckily, we've never experienced much colic with our horses and have had only three deaths caused by it over the years. Since we are situated in the lightning capital of the United States, we actually loose more horses from lightning strikes than we do from colic.

First Wrangler received Joe's standard home remedy for horses suffering from the painful malady: two ounces of bourbon, which is supposed to act as a relaxant. That doesn't seem like much to me for a big animal like a horse, but the idea is to relax it, not make it tipsy!

The second part of the treatment consists of walking the horse to prevent the suffering animal from rolling and to help it to expel the gas. For the human walking the horse, the first part of the treatment is infinitely more pleasant than the exercising part, which can often become long and very tiring after a few hours.

Joe insisted that I go to bed. I dropped off to sleep and woke up about 1:00 a.m. to find Joe still in the barn. Wrangler continued to suffer and Joe was alternating leading him around and sitting in the doorway of the saddle room to rest whenever Wrangler decided to come to a halt for a while. The night air was chilly so I brought coffee, cookies, and a warmer jacket to Joe. After he declined my offer to lead the suffering Wrangler for a while, I went back to bed, but not to sleep.

Finally, at 4:30 I returned to the barn and insisted on "Wrangler walking" for a while so Joe could get some much needed rest.

He reluctantly went into the house and I spent the next twenty minutes or so doing a stint of leading and sitting. At one point Wrangler decided to lay down and I thought I wasn't going to get him onto his feet again! Finally, after I had tugged, begged, and prayed he stood up, albeit reluctantly.

It wasn't very long until my cowboy came back to the barn. "I just couldn't sleep with you out here with Wrangler by yourself," he confessed.

And just then Wrangler flopped down and rolled over before I could stop him. Handling horses really isn't the thing I do best!

So I just stayed at the barn with the two of them. About 6:00, Joe called Doc Smalley, our long-time friend and veterinarian. About that time, Steve arrived to take a hunting party out, and he took a turn walking Wrangler while he waited.

At 7:00 when Doc came, Wrangler was a very sick horse, with a lot of bloating and a rapid heart beat. He wouldn't stand still at all anymore, so we took turns leading him around the barnyard.

After examining him, the diagnosis was "colic and a twisted intestine." Doc's prognosis was "death in six to eight hours."

"Still," he added, "there's always a faint possibility that the shots I gave Wrangler might help him to relax enough for the intestine to unkink."

He didn't really have much hope. . .and neither did we.

There is a surgical procedure that the veterinary department at the University of Florida (ninety miles away) does on colicing horses, but while the cost is reasonable, it is prohibitive except for extremely valuable horses. Since Wrangler was a gelding and valued at $2000, we didn't feel that the cost of the surgery was justified in his case.

That Saturday seemed to drag on forever. Wrangler, sedated and no longer in such great pain, stood tied in the barn with his head hanging low. During the day I continued to return to the barn to look at him. Each time Joe came in the house I greeted him with, "Is there any change?"

Finally, about the middle of the afternoon, he drank a little water, ate a few bites of hay, and most importantly of all, he managed to have a bowel movement. We began to have hope that maybe his intestine *had* unkinked and that he would survive after all.

His condition improved steadily and by the next day he was as well as ever. We were lucky not to lose him but learned a valuable lesson: if the bourbon doesn't relax a horse quick, call the vet!

Although he had rolled and the damage was done before Joe even knew Wrangler had the colic, the shots, if given sooner, could have eliminated a night of suffering for Wrangler, and for Joe!

TRADITIONS

Traditions are a cherished part of every family's life and Christmas has always been the most exciting one of all for our family. With seven youngsters in the house the Christmas season has always been a busy and exciting time for us.

Celebrating Christmas on a ranch is often different from other folks in many ways, especially when the ranch is located far from town, as it is in many areas of the west. Even in heavily populated Florida, ours may differ from city folks, but the spirit of the season is the same.

Decorations have been treasured from year to year, sometimes 'way past the time when their appearance justifies keeping them. Those reminders of the past are part of our Christmas memories and we hold onto them as long as we can, discarding them only when they have reached a stage of dilapidation that can be downright embarrassing when visitors catch a glimpse of them.

In years past Joe and the kids would scout the woods for a cedar tree that would "do," sometimes even putting branches together to form what appeared to be a near-perfect tree. Unless inspected closely, it wasn't at all apparent that it wasn't.

Later, when Christmas tree farms became big business in the area he would take them to visit one several weeks in advance. They enjoyed choosing a tree and "tagging" it with our name. Then, shortly before Christmas, they returned to cut and bring it home. That was almost like going to the woods to hunt one.

After Joe had put it up and placed the lights on it, his job was finished. He never cared much for the actual decorating but enjoyed watching and sharing the fun with the rest of us.

Decorating the tree was always a trip through memory lane. After the silver garland was draped around and around the tree, the ornaments were added. As each one was lifted from the box a chorus of, "Oh, remember the partridge?" Or, "Here's Santa," rang out.

Because our tree didn't go up until a week or less before the big day, it really began to feel like Christmas when the large aromatic cedar tree was finished and standing in all its shining splendor, crowned with the old and cherished star glowing brightly at the very top!

Baking the many different varieties of Holiday cakes and cookies that the family enjoyed only during the Christmas season was a chore both to be dreaded and enjoyed. We made two kinds of fruitcake and four or five different varieties of Christmas cookies each year.

Besides these, made for family and visitors' consumption, there were also the ones to be baked that the kids volunteered for their class parties, and they were good at doing that! One year no less than four little Barthles proudly told me, "I said you would bake cookies for our class party." The parties were all on the same day, but we did it!

The favorite cookie was the "holiday cutouts." Anyone in the house who wanted to (and they all did at sometime or other) helped to roll out, cut out, bake, frost, and decorate them. We usually made enough to fill a *large* boot box!

First, there was the fun of rolling out the chilled dough and cutting out the dozens of cookies. Depending on how many were "helping" at that particular time, a great deal of the counter tops in the kitchen was covered with flour, as well as most of the floor and the assorted kids.

While the cookies were cooling, we made a large bowl of butter frosting and divided it into smaller bowls to be tinted with the various colors needed.

This was all just preliminary; the fun was just beginning! Finally, when all was ready, we all gathered around the big round table to get down to the serious business of decorating cookies. Each tried to outdo the others' artistry.

Santa was clothed in red and white, the green Christmas trees were dotted with colored lights, ribbons and bows were wrapped around colorful presents, and the green mistletoe even had clumps of red berries made of frosting.

There were white angels, yellow stars, and bells of assorted colors. The remaining icing was mixed together to form a more or less brown "mess" to cover the camels and the Rudolphs, who were authentic with their bright red noses. The kids were very artistic and it seemed the enjoyment for them was as much in the making as in the eating. None of the cookies ever went to waste, though, so they must have enjoyed eating them, too.

The highlight of the pre-Christmas activities was the night when the entire family traveled to Tampa, forty miles away, for shopping. We usually went to Zayres, which at the time, was *the* discount store. Actually, as I remember it, Zayres was the only one then.

Once in the store we separated, with Joe taking part of the tribe and me helping the rest. There was a lot of dodging around the aisles and hiding of purchases so the others wouldn't catch a glimpse of what they were getting.

I was more or less elected to be the coordinator. I got to keep the list of who had bought what for whom, and my most important job was to make sure someone didn't duplicate a gift for a sibling who was already receiving the same thing from somebody else. The procedure and responsibility got kind of hectic for me at times as I wrote, marked out, and rewrote the lists!

Even with all of the confusion, it was great fun. When the shopping was over we went to McDonald's for supper. Again, McDonald's was the only fast food chain in our area, and the fastest and least expensive way to feed nine hungry shoppers.

We all looked forward to Christmas shopping together and as the kids got old enough to go on their own, and as the number of those participating grew smaller, I missed them.

Joe and I weren't brave enough to attempt to do any of our shopping that night. We had our own special time for that large and important job.

Wrapping gifts was a lot of

fun for the kids and there was a great deal of shutting doors and cries of "Stay out! I'm wrapping your present!"

Finally, everything was finished and under the tree, ready for Christmas.

Our actual Christmas celebration began after supper on Christmas Eve when we read the Nativity Story and sang carols together. We were hesitantly accompanied on the piano by one girl or another after they started piano lessons.

Reluctantly, the children went to bed, trying to take naps so they would be able to stay awake during Midnight Mass, which actually began at 11:30 with the singing of carols.

For many years one or the other of the kids was either Mary, Joseph, a shepherd, or an angel in the procession at Midnight Mass, and we were required to arrive early enough for the child to be checked out by the Sister and get "lined up."

The kids in school went to Midnight Mass and the younger ones stayed home with a sitter, although most times they woke up when we arrived home. Part of our celebration was "breakfast" after Mass which *always* consisted of the same menu: ham sandwiches, homemade coffee cake, juice and/or ambrosia. With their heads beginning to nod, the kids were ready to go to bed for real after eating. Before that, though, cookies and milk had to be put out as a snack for Santa. Then it was off to bed for them.

Joe and I were lucky to fall into bed by four o'clock and were most often roused soon after five. Even the older, more knowledgeable kids, would wake us excitably demanding that we "see what Santa brought me!"

Watching the joy and wonder on the little faces made all of the work and expense of preparing for the big day a worthwhile effort.

On Christmas, like every other day, the animals on a ranch have to be fed. Joe usually did it by himself on that special day, leaving the boys to enjoy their gifts from Santa.

As soon as we could fit it in between the feeding, we exchanged the gifts each had lovingly prepared for the others. That was quite a sight and Joe and I were usually so engrossed in watching the happy, excited faces that we forgot to open our own gifts until we were reminded, "Open your present and see what I got you."

The climax of the day was dinner, actually a repeat of Thanksgiving since that's what the family wanted. One year I decided I was tired of spending Christmas in the kitchen so Jan, the oldest girl and my right hand at the time, and I prepared meats and salads the day before and announced to all that they could eat whatever and whenever they wanted. We almost had a revolt on our hands! It really wasn't such a good idea and we didn't like the way it worked either so that was the only time we tried that.

So the menu at our house for Christmas invariably stayed the same. New specialties are added to the groaning board occasionally but seldom are the "we always have" favorites dropped. Now that our immediate family numbers fourteen adults and sixteen children, each family brings a dish or dishes to complement the turkey and dressing and other basics which I prepare.

The day was filled with playing, eating, and visits to or from aunts, uncles, and cousins. By early evening everyone, most of all Mom and Dad, were ready for bed!

Now the children are all grown with families of their own. Joe and I finally succumbed to the temptation and purchased what one of the grandsons called a "make-believe" tree. Mark decided when we got it that "It's like hearing that Santa Claus died."

It's pretty, though, with the same, and some new, ornaments each year. The family is used to it now and Joe and I like it.

Just about the only Christmas baking I do now is fruit cakes and the traditional coffee cake that we all share for the after-Mass breakfast at one home or the other.

Joe and I don't suffer from a lack of holiday goodies because all six of "our" girls provide us with them. "What goes around, comes around!"

Christmas dinner and gift exchange is reserved for Papa Joe and Meemaw's house when everyone who is not visiting the family of the spouse gather.

It's interesting to watch sons and daughters make their own traditions with their families. They have taken some from their past, intertwined some from their spouse's family, and thought up some of their own. Each family's celebration is basically the same, but different. I think it is all beautiful.

A Full Table

Florida is blessed with a temperate climate which makes it possible to grow a wide variety of fruit in the front or back yard. The green leaves, colorful blossoms, and delicious fruit provide beauty in the landscaping as well as nutritious food for much of the year.

At various times over the years we have had grapevines, kumquat, grapefruit, tangerine, loquat, and orange trees in our yard. Periodic freezes have leveled them to the ground, but if they didn't sprout back we usually replanted.

We have also tried our luck with pear, plum, peach, and apple trees, usually somewhere in the barn area, in a vain hope that they would be out of harm's way. They never quite made it to production because they were inevitably run over by equipment that was being parked out of the way after use.

Sometimes when we have an excessively large rain fall in a short space of time, the pond rises and floods the yard and barnyard temporarily. When that happens the small trees can be easily killed from standing in the water.

You'd think that with all those trees we'd have been well provided with fruit and nuts but it never has quite worked out that way. There seems to have been a conspiracy among all of the animals in the woods to clean us out! The message passed among the wildlife in the area might have been something like, "Come on over to the Barthle's, they've got a full table for us."

The birds locate and eat the grapes before they become good and ripe. One year I decided I would get the first picking, so I harvested the grapes just before they turned purple and made jelly. It *tasted* like grape jelly, but it sure didn't *look* like grape jelly. . .more like mint!

Next, I tried tying disposable aluminum pie pans in the vines. My scheme was to scare the birds away with the noise of the pans banging against each other. It didn't work that way because the silver brightness of the pans only seemed to attract more birds.

Finally, since the vines were blocking the view of the pond and we weren't reaping the benefit of harvesting any of the grapes anyway, we pulled them out.

In the back yard there are two large pecan trees from which we get very few pecans. The squirrels, and even large crows, consider the trees to be their private banquet table and our pecans a staple in their diets. I have never really begrudged those cute little squirrels a few nuts, but I do wish they weren't so wasteful.

They begin cutting the green pecans and nibbling on them long before they are ripe, or whatever pecans are called when they are ready to fall. The ground under the trees is littered with green pecans for a month or more before they ever start to fall in October. That is, what few the squirrels have left until then!

To appreciate the dilemma we've been in, you have to understand that we live in the middle of the woods and all of the brothers, sisters, aunts, uncles, and cousins of *our* squirrels know about us.

We tried putting tin around the tree trunks to keep the squirrels from climbing the trees. Next, we cut the limbs back from the house and from the trees nearby that we thought were close enough to serve the squirrels as a launching point for jumping into the pecan trees.

But those little critters can *fly*! We hear the pitter-patter of their little feet as they cross the roof to reach the trees, and I have watched them actually *leap* at least fifteen feet up from the roof or a small tree branch to reach the pecan tree.

Then they sit up there chattering at me as they hold one of *my* pecans in their little paws. One day as I stood under the tree, listening to their scolding, something bounced off my head and hit the ground. It was a whole *shelled* pecan! Even though it was comical, and I laughed, I declared that they were adding insult to injury by bombarding me with my own pecans!

It was about that time when we finally gave up. In a vain effort to thin out the squirrel population, Larry shot twenty squirrels that summer. We had a surfeit of squirrel pileau (squirrel and rice) and fried squirrel but still not very many pecan pies!

Now we're resigned to the situation and are just thankful for whatever they are generous enough to let us have and in whatever form we can get it.

The citrus and peach trees are the special territory of the coons and 'possums They love that sweet, juicy fruit! The little varmints climb the trees and eat the insides out of an orange as clean as can be, and then leave the hull hanging there!

One year we had a bumper crop of peaches, so many the limbs broke from the weight of the fruit hanging on them. Each day when I went out to pick the ripe fruit there were very few on the tree but the ground was littered with bare seeds and half-eaten peaches. Undoubtedly, coons must have had their fill of peaches that year but I only got about two pails full.

I don't know if armadillos eat fruit. Their specialty is to feast on caladium and other flower bulbs. They also like to root up the lawn at night and leave tunnels that mark the spot where they've been hunting for something to eat.

Apparently they also think it's great fun to dig a tunnel under the foundation of the house but why they would want to do that is hard to imagine. There's nothing under there but water pipes and maybe some earth worms. We awoke one morning to find a huge hole tapering down to a tunnel going under the foundation of the house. The dogs must have been frantically digging after an armadillo because dirt was thrown everywhere. I filled the hole with water and covered it with dirt but the armadillo must have already gone because we never heard a noise under there.

But those are all small annoyances that have to be endured and laughed at in exchange for the peace and tranquillity of ranch life. For us, we've always figured it was worth it.

SUMMER FUN

Summer in Florida is long, hot, and generally humid. Since swimming is cooling, good exercise and one of our favorite family activities, the children all learned to swim at an early age. First they learned to duck their heads and swim underwater, then managed the dog paddle, and, finally, they mastered the overhead stroke.

One summer I decided to take the younger ones to a free swimming recreational program held by county personnel. I thought they could hone up their swimming skills, get a swimming certificate, and free me from having to watch them in the water and count heads constantly to make sure they were all safe. Our participation didn't last long!

Since it was a structured program there was no flexibility as to which class they were in and no testing to see what their swimming ability was. Larry, the youngest, was placed in the beginner's class where they were learning not to be afraid of the water or of getting their heads wet.

He could already swim under water and was highly indignant that all he was allowed to do was stand waist deep in the water and dunk his head!

Our summer vacation was a week or two in a cottage at Indian Rocks Beach on the Gulf of Mexico. All of the kids loved riding the waves, floating in the salt water, hunting shells, and building sand castles. It didn't matter that the tide would come in and wash away their handiwork. It was cheerfully reconstructed the next day!

Joe doesn't really like the beach and has often said, "I have worked in the sun all my life and I don't want to spend my vacation in it."

I, on the other hand, love the sun and walking on the beach in the heat of the day. So, we worked out a system that allowed each of us to have what we enjoyed.

Joe and the kids would wake up early and go to the beach before it was hot. They would happily play, swim, and build their castles until they figured I had breakfast ready. After they ate, it was my turn to take them back.

After lunch, while everybody rested or took a nap, I could go out to sun or walk alone. Later in the afternoon, after the hottest part of the day was past, we all went back to the beach, even the baby, and played until nearly dark.

Some days were varied and we went bowling or to the movies, played carpet golf, or just rode around for sightseeing.

Staying at the beach, though, was just for a week or two. The Gulf is too far away for us to visit for a casual swim or picnic and the kids liked to swim often from May to October.

At last we bought a fifty foot lot on Lake Lola, five miles from home, and built a screened shed for picnics. Many days after work we took our supper to the lake to swim and eat.

Lake Lola is a pretty, clear lake with a nice white sandy bottom. Three families who are good friends own adjacent lots which, combined, gives us over two hundred feet of lake frontage. It's a wonderful picnic spot for a crowd and through the years, we have enjoyed it both as a group and as individual families.

On many weekends and holidays the four families—plus friends—gathered for a BIG picnic. The men barbecued or fried chicken, grilled hamburgers or hotdogs, or fried mullet fresh from the Gulf. A favorite was corn boiled in its husk and eaten, sweet and dripping with butter and salt.

Sometimes, the women gave the men a break and brought covered dishes of meat, vegetables, salads, and desserts as well as jugs of iced tea, lemonade, or koolade.

The kids from six couples totaled thirty-four. They were 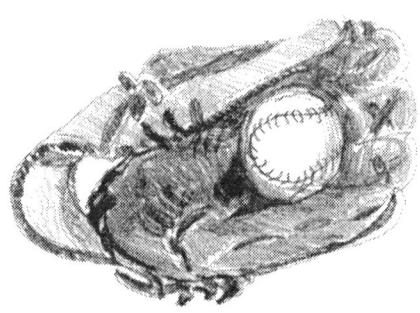 good friends and spent the day jumping off the dock, swimming, riding inner tubes or air mattresses, and playing volley ball. Younger children liked to sit on blankets and play games when they tired of swimming or were forcibly removed from the water to rest. Babies and toddlers were content in strollers, walkers, or play pens.

The men enjoyed horseshoes, volleyball, or just resting and conversing.

As the kids grew older they became interested in learning to water ski and so boats became part of the scene.

They really got quite good at it and could ski barefoot, on one foot, double and, finally, in a pyramid.

One Fourth of July the youngsters staged a water show for us. Late in the afternoon after most of the other boats on the lake had retired for the day, we all lined our lawn chairs up close to the shore to view the show.

After performing all of their specialties for us, their finale was a pyramid of teenaged boys skiing past in perfect precision. Proud parents that we were, we thought they compared favorably with the performers at Cypress Gardens!

But another Fourth of July almost didn't turn out so well.

Randy was entered in the calf roping at the Kissimmee rodeo and was up on the Fourth. Joe was with him and I took the rest of the bunch to the picnic at the lake.

Naturally, when we got there, the kids all jumped out of the car and ran straight to the water. As was my habit, I immediately started counting the heads of my children.

As I stood there watching, three year old Mark was bobbing up and down and, as I thought, waving at me. I waved back and shouted, "I see you."

After this went on for a couple of times it suddenly dawned on me that he wasn't waving at me. I could see that he was in trouble and started for the water in a run!

Luckily one of the men spied him at the same time and, being nearer, waded in and pulled the limp little boy out before I got to him.

It wasn't funny at the time, but in retrospect I laughed and wondered how many mothers have stood by and watched their child drown—waving cheerily to them as they did!

BRING 'ER ON IN

Cow working time! The time on a cattle ranch for gathering, vaccinating, neutering, worming, pregnancy checking, marking, and branding. It's long, hot days of work for the crew, including the boys and girls of the family. And, then, after the weary day is over there's still feeding to be done when they finally get home, many times long after dark.

The work in the cowpens goes on sometimes even in the rain, and although everybody prefers not to work while it's lightning, even that is necessary at times to get the job finished.

The pens are always either dusty or muddy; there's hardly an in-between. Either way, it makes for some pretty filthy clothes that you can smell coming.

For the ranch wife, who doesn't help with the actual labor, cow work means packing lunches, late suppers, and the impossibly dirty clothes in her laundry room. As one who has done more than I consider to be my fair share of laundering a large ranch family's dirty clothes, I think I can qualify as an expert on the subject.

As bad as dusty pens are, I'll opt for them over muddy ones when it comes to the clothes worn in them. There's not much worse to wash than jeans and shirts that have spent the day in the mud and manure of a wet cow pen. At the end of a hard day's work, cowboys sure do clean up a lot quicker and better than their clothes do! Of course the towels they use after their showers show a lot of the grime, too.

I've always had an idea, a hope anyway, that there must be a special corner in heaven reserved for Moms who wash cowboy work clothes and football, basketball, and baseball uniforms!

There are a lot of ranch wives who help with cow work. That was never a part of my job description, I'm sorry to say. As much as I would have liked to do it, I couldn't be in two places at once, and my priority was to have and care for the babies.

I rode some with Joe when we were first married, at the tail end of screw-worm days in Florida. That was mostly just walking the horses through woods and pastures, looking for infected cattle and doctoring them. At least, Joe did. I watched, and handed him the medicine.

One day, as we were riding along, we spied a cow in the distance that Joe didn't think looked just right, so we rode over to check her out. She looked as if she had some kind of big growth on the bottom of her face, top and bottom.

As we got close to her we could make out that the poor thing had a gopher shell wedged over her mouth holding it shut so that she couldn't graze or drink water.

In Florida, a gopher is not the fuzzy little creature found in many areas of the country. Our gopher is a member of the tortoise or turtle family and is a land turtle. They are docile creatures that have short club-shaped feet and blunt claws that are not useful for fighting. They are slow and clumsy and need protection from their enemies, which is probably why they dig "gopher holes" to live in. The holes are really a long sloped tunnel which, incidentally, rattlesnakes like to live in, too.

The only protection the gopher has is its shell, the bones of which are closely joined and the head, legs, and tail can be drawn into it. The outside is sometimes covered with scales. This shell was what was stuck on the cow's mouth and causing the trouble.

Joe roped her, and after a little difficulty, succeeded in removing the shell from the cow. He finished the job by doctoring the screwworms before removing the rope and turning her loose.

Riding was one of the things I would have liked to do more often. I was always thankful that I never took a fall, probably because of the gentle horses which I chose to ride.

My last experience of penning cows cured me of pining to help. The younger kids were all in school and I was earnestly assured by my cowboy husband that it was really a necessity for me to help pen some cows.

"We're shorthanded," I was told.

I knew that 'most anybody could "plug up a hole" and our little kids helped, so surely I could do the job! I agreed to go.

Feeling very much needed, I rode out with Joe and whichever of the older sons were home at the time. I was given my instructions: "We'll bring them out of the woods and start them into the pens. You can bring up the ones that cut back on us."

Right then I began to get a sneaking suspicion that I wasn't needed as I had been led to believe.

"All right," I thought. "I can manage my assignment."

Maybe.

In my mind I had visions of a fairly large bunch of cattle cutting back to get past me and return to the scrub they had just been rousted from. I visualized riding my horse at a full run, reining, and turning him to cut the strays back to the herd. I would show them all that I could do it, and do it with style!

How mistaken could one ambitious, inexperienced, would-be cowgirl be? I was posted out in the middle of an open pasture while all of the other riders went into the scrub oaks to bring out the cattle. I think the reason I didn't ask why I couldn't go with them was because I was told I was needed where they put me. For what I wasn't sure, and never did find out.

Another factor might have been that I didn't have a cow whip, didn't know how to make one pop anyway, couldn't yell very loud, and couldn't whistle at all. Maybe all of those deficiencies disqualified me from taking part. Still, they knew all of that before they asked me to come along.

I could hear the others whooping and whistling, and having a good ole time as they made a sweep through the woods and brought the critters out. Arriving in the open field, they bunched the cattle up and rushed them into the holding pen.

In that whole big expanse of pasture the only thing left was just me and one old crippled cow. Joe had managed to shout over his shoulder, as they rushed the herd to the pens, "Bring 'er on in!"

I did. For those who have never pushed a string haltered cow, I can tell you that it takes a while and a lot of patience to do. She would take a few steps and I would think, "At last we are going." And we would, for a few more steps. Then she would stop and I would urge her on again. This process was repeated over and over again, all the way to the pens. . .three-quarters of a mile away.

I think it would have been easier to rope, tie, and load that poor old crippled critter onto a trailer or a front-end loader and haul her in. I've always had a sneaking suspicion that if I hadn't been there, they could have figured out *some* way to get her to the pens in less time than it took to walk her in.

And, secretly, I thought that they knew she was there and used me to save themselves some time and trouble!

A CONFESSION

It was a hot Sunday morning and I had just finished dressing for church when the quiet of the morning was shattered suddenly by the high-pitched trumpeting and snorting of two horses who were obviously fighting.

When I raced out the back door, I found our two stallions fighting across the fence of the little pasture behind the house.

Dude, the older one, was in the pasture and Tiger, who had somehow escaped from the barn, was in the yard. He was looking for trouble and Dude was more than willing to take the youngster on and teach him who was boss!

I wasn't sure if Joe was around but, not knowing what else to do I yelled for him. Gratefully, I heard him call back from the direction of the barn, "I'm coming!"

Joe has never liked to run; he's a typical cowboy who doesn't even care for walking! He proudly admits that he hates to walk and loves to ride and has often said, "I'd walk two miles to catch a horse to ride one mile." I believe he would.

But that morning he was really putting out, coming at a trot which for him has always been equal to at least a gallop in a horse.

He had grabbed a rope and was building a loop in it as he came. As he hurriedly explained it to me, the idea was for the two of us to hem Tiger up so Joe could put a rope on him and lead him back to the barn, rather than to try to chase him back.

Tiger didn't show any indication of wanting to leave and apparently the only thing to do was to rope and pull him away from Dude.

Tiger also didn't want nor intend for us to do that. After trotting back and forth along the fence a few times, he suddenly lunged in my direction, which he obviously considered to be the most likely avenue of escape.

As he was headed directly towards me in a good run, I was supposed to step out in front of him and *he* was supposed to turn back. Joe was waiting behind him with his coiled rope, looped and ready to throw.

I hesitated just long enough for the running horse to dash around me while my cowboy was commanding in a loud voice to, "Go ahead. He'll stop!"

Well, I didn't. . .and he didn't.

While all of this action was taking place on the yard side of the fence, Dude was running up and down on the pasture side, whinnying and making all the noises which stallions make when they are squaring up for a fight.

Tiger, apparently gaining courage from having eluded his two human adversaries, decided to have another go at Dude, who was quite evidently ready to respond. The morning air was filled with their snorts and squeals as they tried to bite, paw, and kick each other across the fence. At one point both horses reared up over the board fence, which was topped with barbed wire.

Their powerful muscles rippled as they balanced on their hind legs, pawing and biting each other. Dude's chestnut and Tiger's sorrel coats glistened as the sun's rays caught and reflected the moisture of their sweat.

It was a beautiful scene, but dangerous for them if one or both had come down on top of the fence. Luckily, each returned to earth safely on his own side and neither was injured.

Joe was still trying to maneuver into position to put a noose around Tiger's neck, who wasn't being at all cooperative. Each time Joe got within throwing distance, Tiger would break off the fight and move on.

Finally the fight worked its way around to the front of the yard where Tiger decided he'd had all of the fighting he wanted. He loped off down the lane as Dude trumpeted his challenge to "Come back and fight!"

The scenario at that point was: Tiger galloping swiftly down the lane, Joe, still carrying his rope, was following on foot and me, slightly handicapped in my high heeled shoes, racing to bring the car.

By the time I had backed it out of the driveway, picked up Joe, and caught up with Tiger, he was three-quarters of a mile away and almost to the hard road where even on a Sunday morning there's quite a bit of traffic.

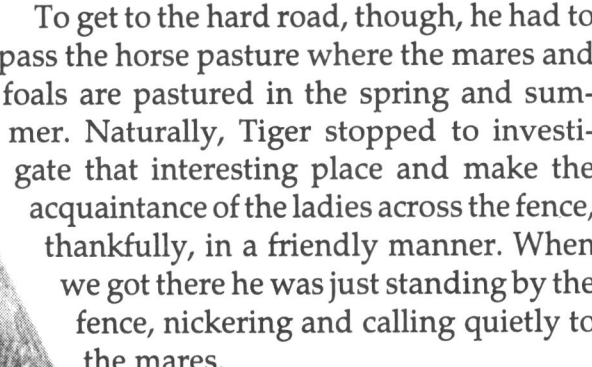

To get to the hard road, though, he had to pass the horse pasture where the mares and foals are pastured in the spring and summer. Naturally, Tiger stopped to investigate that interesting place and make the acquaintance of the ladies across the fence, thankfully, in a friendly manner. When we got there he was just standing by the fence, nickering and calling quietly to the mares.

I was able to get around him there to block his way to the hard road in case he wanted to make another dash for freedom. But, tired from his fight and run, he was willing to have the rope placed around his neck. Quickly fashioning it into a halter, Joe wearily started out to lead him home. Bringing up the rear in the car, I felt I should have been the one leading Tiger because, after all, I'm the walker in the family.

On the way to church, after apologizing for not turning Tiger back in the yard, I reminded Joe, "You stepped in front of a running horse one time not too many years ago and wound up with a broken ankle."

I got a typical cowboy response to that kind of remark: no comment. Complete silence.

Encouraged, I admitted something I never had before: I'm afraid of horses. Oh, I know that most of them are gentle and easy to handle, but they're so BIG!

"I don't think I could force myself to step out in front of a running horse, unless you or one of the children were in danger," I confessed. And then, as an afterthought, I added, "And I'm not sure I could make myself do it for you either."

It was lucky that Tiger escaped from the barn before we left for church. If the fight had happened while no one was at home, we might have returned to find two injured stallions.

We had been ready for church a little early that morning, which was unusual for us, so Joe had time to shower and change clothes before we went. And we made it with a minute to spare!

A ROADSIDE VIEW

Florida has long been a Utopia for retired people, especially those from the northeastern states, who have chosen to spend their golden years in the land of sunshine and beauty.

More and more of the population moving into the state, however, are young and middle-aged families who have been transferred by the firms for which they work. Some are simply making a life or career change and choose Florida in which to start again.

For whatever reasons, people flock to Florida and it makes for a lot of congested, overpopulated areas. Many people who live in subdivisions or condominiums don't have much chance to view nature. We have a whole generation of children growing up with no exposure to, nor knowledge of, what the countryside looks like, where their food comes from, nor anything about animals in the wild. These families get a lot of pleasure from driving through the countryside to look at the scenery and wildlife.

Retired agricultural people must enjoy the chance to get back out in the country for a little while. Many times we see couples or families who have parked under a shade tree by the side of the road, sitting on camp stools or a blanket, enjoying a picnic lunch.

For some time our ranch has been a point of interest in this area for people driving by. Several things contribute to this interest.

Sometimes it is my duty and privilege to chauffeur a load of the grandchildren to St. Anthony School, the same school that one of their parents and grandparents attended. As I was parked by the side of the hard road one morning waiting for the last of my passengers to congregate, an out-of-state couple stopped and asked me if I knew what the purpose was of the "large wire pens" in the pasture.

I was able to explain to them that it was an experiment by the Extension Service to test different kinds of fertilizer on Bahia grass. The purpose, of course, was to identify the fertilizer with the most efficient ingredients to grow the most nutritious grass for the cattle to graze. They were also testing to determine the best time or times of the year to apply the fertilizer.

That satisfied the people because as they drove away they said, "That's all we wanted to know. Thank you."

People also like to stop and watch the bulls, mares, and foals in the "hold-up" pasture by the side of the hard road. All of the pastures have descriptive names that identify them to the family: Gator Pond, Sawgrass, Scrub, and so on.

I suddenly realized recently that I had never heard the origin of the name of the hold-up pasture even though it has been called that since before I married into the family.

Joe explained, "It's the pasture where we used to "hold up" cows with screwworms that needed a lot of doctoring."

Ask, and you shall learn!

In the fall and winter, the bulls are pastured in that pasture and in the spring and summer the mares and foals have possession of it.

Passers-by also show a lot of curiosity about the old cast iron bathtubs that are lined up in the pasture. Until he accumulated as many as he needed, Joe used to search junk yards and the wrecking sites of old houses for them. He then placed them in the pasture to hold feed and shelled corn for the bulls.

As my cowboy explained *that*, "They are cheap, durable, and heavy enough so that the bulls can't push them around. Then, when the ground around the tubs gets wallowed out or muddy, we just hook up to them with a truck or tractor and pull them to a new, clean spot for the bulls to stand in as they eat."

City folks, though, might find it a strange sight to see a

row of bathtubs in a pasture with cattle lined up on either side of them! Maybe they think we provide facilities for our cattle to take baths!

But the thing that has drawn the most interest has been the Sandhill Whoopers. These big birds have always remained on the flats about five miles down in the pasture. For the last few years, when the bulls are in the hold-up pasture, the Whoopers move up next to the hard road.

Our theory is that they like the whole kernel corn that gets spilled and that is also in the bull droppings. Many people have returned with their binoculars and cameras, both still and video, to capture the birds on film.

As I watch the Whoopers I find myself thinking, "Isn't it amazing how animals and birds can communicate with each other to spread the word that, "There's food available about five miles from here. Let's go get it!"

These birds also feed on army worms during a heavy infestation, as do the white Asian Egrets. Sometimes the entire pangola grass hay field will appear to be a sea of white waves as the Egrets constantly move around while feasting on the army worms.

If the infestation is not too heavy the Egrets and the Whoopers clean it up for us. At other times it is necessary to have the field sprayed in order to save the grass so it will grow to make hay later.

The Egrets also like to have a free ride on the backs of the cattle, maybe to eat ticks or lice form them. It's too bad they don't come equipped with night lights so they could work on the mole crickets when they emerge from the ground at night. Those little boogers can literally destroy a pasture in no time! During one year we lost 500 acres of pasture grass to them. Since they destroy the roots, all that was left was bare ground which had to be replanted.

Our Whooping Cranes are not the ones that are almost extinct in the United States but, like them, the Sandhill Whoopers have a loud raucous whoop that can be heard a mile or so away as they lift clumsily in flight or swoop down for a heavy landing.

Even though these birds are called the Florida Crane they also reside in South Georgia. For those who are interested in that sort of thing, their scientific name is *G.C. Praetensis*.

Standing about three feet high with a wing spread of approximately six feet, they are gray with a small patch of bare red skin on their foreheads. They like to eat small plants, insects, frogs, worms, reptiles, small fish, and the eggs of other animals. And as we know, they like corn!

During the mating season, groups of them gather to dance crazily and hop excitably into the air. Joe said he has watched them perform their mating rites and he found it to be really interesting to see.

At other times, I suppose when they have their craws full, the cranes stand lazily on one leg with their heads drawn back on their shoulders.

I have heard that the cranes mate for life. They build their nests in bushes or marshes and the female lays only a few eggs. Maybe that's why there are so few of them! They are legally protected but between the small supply of eggs and the varmints destroying their nests, they can't have too much of a population increase.

For several years we had a visitor who came every few days. He would drive down the dirt road, park his car, and just sit and watch the cattle, horses and wildlife. In talking with him we discovered he was a farmer from the north who had retired to Florida.

He kept his practiced farmer's eye on things for us, too, and spotted things that were amiss. One day he told Joe he had seen a horse in the pasture up the road that had been cut. When Joe investigated there was, indeed, a horse with a cut, it needed a tetanus shot, and Joe appreciated the help.

All of a sudden we missed Mr. Quakenbush—that really was his name. At least he said it was and we believed him. He just stopped coming and we never did know what happened to him. We missed his visits, though, and hope that wherever he is there are some cattle and horses for him to watch.

A NATURE WATCH

Eventually, as happens in all families, all of the children were "out of the nest." Or as much out of it as could be expected while the majority of them still live within a few miles of each other and work together as part of a family operation. As it should, home remains the place where they go to look for something to snack on or drink, or to borrow a needed article.

With no one to harry and hurry into getting ready for church, Sunday became my special time to loaf, at least for a little while in the morning. Joe is out feeding his horses and riding around in his pickup, checking pumps, fences, cattle, gates, grass, or whatever he thinks needs to be done. It's his method of relaxing and getting his plans prioritized for the coming week's work.

I try to sleep until about eight o'clock, or until the sounds of croaking rain frogs, bellowing bulls, or chirping crickets finally pierce my consciousness to rouse me. Then, still drowsy with my eyes heavy-lidded from sleep, I settle myself on the front porch with a cup of steaming coffee and indulge in my weekly nature watch.

While I sit there and watch the wildlife in our yard, I can dreamily relax, think out worrisome problems, reflect on life's blessings, and just generally recharge my emotional batteries.

There's usually two or three squirrels playing tag up, down, and around the oak trees. Now and then Al the cat spies them and summons up enough energy to chase one of them up a tree. Actually, Al's a very good hunter when she sets her mind to it. She often drags the remains of her kill to leave by the back door as a mute reminder that we most probably need her more than she needs us!

I have watched squirrels bury pecans in the flower bed by the porch, which is quite a distance from where they found them. We have little pecan trees sprouting up all over the yard from pecans being "squirreled" away for a rainy day. It's a mystery why the hiders didn't go back for their nuts after they had taken the trouble to bury them. Maybe they forgot where they put them, or perhaps they just never needed to eat them!

As I sit there peacefully sipping my coffee, I keep an eye on the birds as they chirp, twitter, scratch in the grass, and make quick darts from branch to branch on the trees and azalea bushes. They seem to have unlimitless energy and are seldom still for very long.

There's a pretty good variety of them: wrens, sparrows, cardinals, blue jays, mocking birds, and even some redheaded woodpeckers whose rapid-fire attack on trees or fence posts punctuates the relative quiet of the Sabbath morning. I reflect that it's unfair that the males are the prettiest of the species while the female is the plain one. We can be thankful this isn't the case in the human race where looks are equal: the male is handsome and the female is pretty!

If I stay quiet enough I can occasionally catch sight of a hummingbird hovering just outside the screen with its tiny wings whirring faster than the eye can see. I sit and gaze, fascinated, until it tires and darts away.

Once, long ago, I heard a rustling in the flower bed. Three armadillos, babies or possibly half grown, were rooting around in a search for something to eat. Their mother wasn't anywhere near so she must have considered them to be old enough to wander on their own.

Armadillos are a small American mammal whose name in Spanish means "little armored thing." They have bony shells and strong claws which they use to dig tunnels in the ground in which they live.

Their snouts are long and narrow and they use their tongue to lick up insects. Since they have only small back teeth, they cannot bite in self-defense and their shell is their best protection.

The armadillo's shell, made of many small parts of horny armor fitted closely together, is hard and stiff but jointed across the back. This design allows it to curl up into a hard tight ball with the shell on the outside and its head and feet tucked safely on the inside. Consequently, few animals are able to get a grip on the armadillo with their teeth or claws and do this only as a last resort.

Full-grown Armadillos are about two feet long, including its tail, but those youngsters were much smaller and their armor was still pinkish colored, not gray as it would be when they were adults and weigh about five pounds.

Since I wasn't afraid that they would bit me, I captured all three of them by the simple method of picking them up by their tails and placing them in a box until Joe came home. In my naiveté, I asked him to return them to the woods. He did take them to the woods but, in retrospect, I very seriously doubt that he turned them loose! Armadillos are bad about tearing up quail nests which are made on the ground, and eating the eggs.

The neighbor's Red Angus Cattle graze placidly in a pasture directly in front of our house. Our bulls are near and in a little field adjoining the hard road, there's almost always a horse or two. They alternate grazing with racing swiftly back and forth in the small area, making sharp turns and coming to skidding stops as they whinny shrilly.

As I stand in the office and look out the back window, I can watch the fish as they jump and break the still surface of the lake. Sometimes ducks and Canadian geese gently float on the surface; at other times they voice raucous cries as they settle on the water or launch themselves into flight.

I especially like to see the long-necked "snake" birds as they dive from the air or the limb of a dead tree that stands in the edge of the water as they attempt to catch a fish for their breakfast.

Occasionally, I sight a snake in the yard, but not often. When I do, it's usually a black racer, an indigo or "gopher" snake, or what we call chicken or oak snakes. I long ago decided that if they don't bother me, I won't bother them so we coexist quite peacefully.

Poisonous snakes are absolutely something else! I've only spied one coral, one puffadder, one ground rattler, two diamond back rattlers, and what I assumed was a cotton mouth moccasin. That's not too bad in forty-four years but it's more than enough for me!

I enjoy my Sunday morning nature watch. Joe comes in, relaxed and hungry, from his morning jaunt, and we have breakfast before going to church. No matter how busy the rest of the day may turn out to be, it's a pleasant and peaceful way to start a Sunday.

I'M A FLORIDA COWBOY

Years ago someone suggested that I write a poem to send to the Cowboy Poet's Jamboree, or something like that. At that time I had never heard of Baxter Black or any of the other Cowboy Poets and I didn't even know what a "cowboy poet" was. Nevertheless, I wrote something and sent it in. I never heard anything from anyone about it and more or less forgot all about it.

I used our sons as a model for it. They, to me, typify today's Florida Cowboy.

I'm a Florida cowboy, born and bred,
From the soles of my boots to the hat on my head.
From the day I was born this ranch has been home,
And far from here I don't want to roam.

I'll tell you my tale, I'll tell you my story,
Though I haven't much fame and I haven't much glory.
I was born to a cowboy and his city-bred wife,
Horses and cattle have made up my life.

I rode with my Dad before I could walk,
I took my first spill before I could talk.
I had my own horse before I was three,
A cowboy was all I ever hoped I would be.

I rode in the pickup to check on the cows,
And drove the jeep when I had learned how.
We penned the cows, we marked them and branded,
I HAD to help 'cause we were always shorthanded.

I learned about soil and grasses each day,
I went to the field and helped to make hay.
I drove the tractor to mow, disk, and chop,
And built and patched fences 'til I thought I would drop.

I did all the things that other boys do,
Played baseball and football and basketball, too.
I joined 4-H and showed some fat steers,
In FFA I was on livestock and meat teams for years.

I went off to college where I judged some more,
And learned Animal Science—that sure was a chore.
Some of those city boys sure did act strange,
And my heart was always at home on the range.

I came home and married a city girl, too,
We had us some kids, what else could we do?
We're still raising cattle and horses so fine,
I may not have much, but at least it's all mine.

I'm a Florida cowboy, born and bred,
I stand on my own, I'm not easily led.
I work hard and play hard and give thanks to the Lord,
For my life on this ranch, I give you my word.